VOCABULARY OF DIALECTS
SPOKEN IN THE
NICOBAR AND ANDAMAN ISLES

WITH A
SHORT ACCOUNT OF THE NATIVES,
THEIR CUSTOMS AND HABITS,
AND OF PREVIOUS
ATTEMPTS AT COLONISATION

FR. AD. DE ROEPSTORFF

SECOND EDITION

ISBN : 978-93-5324-577-1 (HB)

First Published, 1875

Published, 2020

Published by

Facsimile Publisher
12 Pragati Market
Ashok Vihar, Ph-2
Delhi-110052
E-mail: books@facsimilepublisher.com

Printed at: G. Print Process, Delhi.

Vocabulary of Dialects
Spoken in the Nicobar and Andaman Isles

Author: FR. AD. DE Roepstorff

HENRICO RINKIO, Ph.D.,

Regi Daniae a consiliis justitiae,
Mercaturae Groenlandicae praefecto,
Cujus laetum vultum et benignum animum puer vidi,
prudentiam juvenis perspexi,

Qui primus de insulis Nicobaricis librum scripsit,
Cujus, dum erunt qui de illis scribant, nulla oblivio
Memoriam delebit, quamvis ille aliam gloriam
ex ultimo septentrione tulerit,

Hunc libellum summa observantia summoque
studio praeditus

D D D

F. A. de RÖEPSTORFF,

In universitate Hauniensi candidatus philosophiae,
Societatis regiae antiquariorum septentrionalium sodalis.

VOCABULARY OF DIALECTS

SPOKEN IN THE

NICOBAR AND ANDAMAN ISLES.

My reasons for writing this *Vocabulary* have been as follows:— *(1st,)* to enable officers deputed on duty to the Nicobars to keep up communication with this truly remarkable people, and *(2nd,)* especially I wish to secure to the scientific world the languages of these people, who are fast dying out. Several small collections have been at different times made, from which I have extracted only a few words that were unknown to me, and which have been noted in every case. The first collection of words of the Nancowry dialect was made by Surgeon Fontana, who was there from April to September 1778 in an Austrian vessel, the *Joseph and Theresa.* The next was made by the Revd. D. Rosen, a Danish clergyman, who was there from August 1831 till December 1834: he saw a good deal of the natives and was a general favorite with them. It is to be regretted that when his house was burnt at Nancowry most of his papers were destroyed, but in his *Erindringer fra mit Ophold pau de Nikobarske Öer Kjöbenhavn* (Copenhagen, 1839,) he gives sixty-three words in addition to the numerals. In 1846 a few words were collected by Father Barbe, a French priest from the Straits of Malacca, who came on a flying visit in his own little schooner, the *Carolina.* He was accompanied by M. Lacrampe, who had stayed on Teressa Island as a missionary, and was thus able to obtain the best information about the islands. The Commander of the Danish Government Steamer *Ganges* gave them a passage in his ship, (which was at the time at Little Nicobar,) to Teressa and Katchall Islands, where M. Lacrampe landed to take away some property left behind by the French Mission a short time before. Dr. Rink, the present director of the Greenland trade, who was a member of the Galatea Expedition, has written a paper on the geology of the islands, and mentions a few Nicobarese words. He came there in December

in its home. At the Andamans a similar tribe is spoken of, but I think its existence a myth. At the Nicobars the islands are so extensive that an inland people could subsist; but it is not so at the Andamans. I hope, however, to be able to search for these Shobængs before very long.

THE NANCOWRY PEOPLE. I have now done with the foreigners, as I term them, and turn to the Nancowry people whom I know best, and of whom I have seen a good deal, having spent a year and a quarter among them. This part of the *Vocabulary* was commenced during my first stay there, and in the interval between my first and second residence Mr. E. H. Man, an Assistant on the Port Blair Establishment, made his collection.

Where they live. The Nancowry people, as I call them, inhabit Trinkut, Nancowry, Camorta, Katchall, Car Nicobar and the coasts of Little and Great Nicobars. They may also inhabit Teressa and Bompoka; but I do not know, as I have not visited these islands. It would, however, appear from the *Vocabulary* of M. Plaisant that they are pure Nancowry people. This race is well worth the trouble of a closer investigation. They display a high degree of civilisation. Though it is about as democratic a state of society as could well be imagined, they are still strictly governed by their old rules and customs. Nowhere is property safer than there. I cannot make

Origin. out their origin, but I am certain that they are not Burmese, and I do not believe that they are related to the Malays; I have reason to suspect that the so-called aborigines of Formosa are nearer related to them than any of their neighbours. This is, however, a suggestion only (vide *The Mail*, September 7th, 1874, Formosa). I believe them to be an ancient people who have preserved their old civilisation and religious customs intact, while perhaps their religious ideas and theories have gradually died out. Each one can do what he or she likes, but within certain limits. The climate is so mild and the land so rich, that they have everything they require; luxuries only are supplied by foreigners, and doubtless it would be best for them to have no intercourse with any foreigners at all. They inhabit only the low alluvial coast, where there is a reef to shelter their village, and where cocoanuts grow. The

Cocoanuts. cocoanut tree is their great mine of wealth. The young nut provides a cool, sweet drink, far more wholesome than the water obtainable, which contains decomposed matter. The ripe nut forms an important part of their diet; their dogs, fowls, and pigs live almost entirely on it. Traders visit these islands solely for the cocoanuts. The cocoanut tree also supplies them with palm wine and water vessels. The cocoanut yields oil, which they know how to extract; the dry leaves make beautiful torches, which burn well and are used while fishing. The bread made from the fruit of the

Pandanus Mellori. *Pandanus Mellori* is much eaten; and fish they can obtain at all seasons. The *Pandanus* grows to perfection in this warm, moist climate and in a half-swampy soil. It requires, however, great labor to extract and cook the edible farinaceous part. The process

Cycas. of extracting the fibre is very tedious work. A species of *Cycas*

also yields a farinaceous material, which is eaten; but the *Cycas* is not cultivated, as it grows so slowly, that it is rare. The forest yields capital timber for the posts and planks of their houses, and for boats. The bark of a small tree makes very good twine and fishing-lines, and the jungles abound in rattan, which they use for the tying of planks, making baskets, and the like. Wild hog abounds, and the jungles contain very few obnoxious animals. On none of the islands are found deadly poisonous snakes, except on Teressa. The people describe this snake as black and making a hissing noise. The worst thief on these islands is a big boa, or rather a python (*Schneideri*), which steals fowls and small pigs.

Timber. Fibre. Rattan. Snakes. *Python Schneideri.*

The *Areca* (betel-nut tree) and the *Chavica* (betel-leaf) are very common, and are cultivated. In the creeks in the Nancowry group and in Sambelong (*i. e.*, Great and Little Nicobars) the *Nipa fructicans* grows, which affords a good thatching material for the houses, (in Car Nicobar the lalang grass is used instead). The sea abounds in fish, which the Nancowry people spear at night by torch-light from their light canoes. They use also baskets, which are sunk with little stones and left for a couple of nights under water. Nets and stakes they do not use, but often fishing-lines. The crabs and the crayfish are very large, and oysters are found in some places in the southern islands. Turtles they are fond of eating, and the tortoise is also caught. Sharks and alligators are the worst of their sea and water enemies. Their boats are, however, very safe, and it is thirty years since any one was eaten by an alligator.

Nipa fructicans. Lalang grass. Fish. Mode of catching fish.

I think I have shown the resources this people possess, and that they have all that a people in their state can want,—food, good and plentiful; excellent materials for building houses and making boats; a hot, moist climate, the heat seldom much above or much under 85° Fahrenheit. Can it be wondered at that they give way to the temptations offered to them to lead a lazy life? I hope, however, to show that the Nancowry people, though they love to be lazy and to stretch themselves in the shade to sleep, are nevertheless very active when they have anything to do. And what they do, they do well.

The villages are built on the low land below the jungle, and are generally situated behind a coral reef, to be sheltered from the sea. In a village there are rarely more than twenty houses, and often only two or three. The houses of the Nancowry people and their way of living remind me of what I have read of the remains of villages found in the Swiss lakes, and perhaps many things could be explained, from a knowledge of the Nancowry people, which now are doubtful.

Their villages.

The houses are raised on poles some six or eight feet from the ground and stand below high-water mark, so that the water washes under them when the tide comes in and clears away whatever refuse may be collected underneath them,—which, however, is not very much, as each thing has its place, even refuse. Underneath the houses are little rough platforms on which *Pandanus* fruit, not prepared, is kept. There lie also the troughs for feeding the dogs and

Their houses raised on poles below high-water mark.

swine, and there sits the woman of the house every evening about 5 o'clock and feeds her live-stock,—pigs, fowls, and savage dogs. There are also the hencoops. The houses do not look very nice outside as they are weather-beaten, the rains being very heavy for six months and the winds very high; but when you enter a hut, you will invariably find it well-made, well-kept, and in beautiful order. A little square hole in the floor gives entrance, and on the landing-place there lies a little brush (one of the scales of the *Pandanus*) to wipe your feet with, so as not to bring sand or mud on the floor: I have never seen dust or sand on a floor in any village. Right in front of the landing-place on the other side of the hut is the fire-place. This is a long rectangular railed-off place, with a platform above it. In this is cooked all that is wanted. The 'larome' or *Pandanus* bread must be well boiled; but otherwise the cookery is very primitive. On both sides of the cooking-place are poles hung some four or five feet from the floor with cocoanut shells polished and cleaned inside, quite black. These are the water cisterns of the people. They are called 'hishoje.' Above the cooking-place are hung the unfinished shells, and also 'larome' ready for eating, neatly tied up in leaves.

Cleanliness.

Cooking-place.

Pigs' jaws.

Looking back to the entrance again, you find a row or two of some pigs' lower jaws with big tusks. It has been generally surmised that these represented wild boars killed by the master of the house and a sort of proof of his valour, and I expect it was so in former times. Now-a-days they are those of pigs reared in the house, and the woman who can show the biggest is the proudest. All the domestic animals, as well as the cooking utensils, belong entirely to the housewife. Above the pigs' teeth are rows of spears of different sorts; along the inside of the house-wall are boxes and mats, and the middle of the floor is kept clean and clear. As a rule, you will find big figures, cut in wood in natural size, in the middle of the floor representing men in European dress. More than once have I started, on going up into a house, at a man standing ready to strike me; and I have found it to be one of these figures. They do not worship idols, but still they like to have images of all sorts about the house. As a rule, one or two figures are tied to the roof, and hang down about five feet from the floor. These figures are of every description. Sometimes a ship in full-rig and the captain with a speaking-trumpet or a telescope in his hand. The ship is made to rest on a fish of great size; very often the fish has the head of an alligator. The roof of the house is like a cupola, and is made with beautiful regularity. A grating is constructed so as to cut off the upper part of the dome, and there are kept the things they want well preserved or well smoked; for, as there is no funnel for the smoke, it has to strain out through the roof and leave all the soot behind. The grating is therefore, as a rule, black. This round cupola-shape presents the least resistance to the wind and rain, and gives more room than square-built houses would afford. Several villages have, however, lately been burnt by English men-of-war; in such villages you will find many square-shaped houses. At a distance, the round houses resemble bee-hives.

Domestic affairs belong to the wife.

Images, not idols.

On both sides of the village the boats, or rather canoes, lie. These are very light, and are carried up high-and-dry as soon as work is done. The canoes are made of one piece of wood, hollowed out and burnt, always very carefully made. The canoes are flat-bottomed and big-bellied, but narrow above, with a little raised rail, and small sticks are laid across at regular intervals to sit on. They have an outrigger and are fast-sailing and very safe when managed with care. The bow protrudes so far that a man can stand on it with his spear. Their war canoes have got a peculiarly-formed ornament some ten feet above the bow, like a figure-head ornamented with dragons. Their canoes.

Where the reef allows the boats to come near to the village, some high poles are raised, with knots of leaves tied all the way up; these leaves are green when the poles are raised. Village posts.

The dress of the people is scanty, only so much as decency demands. The men have a narrow strip, two inches broad, hanging down behind like a tail, and the women wear a little blue skirt. Vanity has however there, as elsewhere, its worshippers. The greatest prize in dress is a black silk hat, and many an old man appears when he wants to be grandest with an old silk hat and his little strip of cloth. For a woman a skirt sewed after the European fashion is a treasure. The usual thing was to see the whole village turn out and dress when my boat approached. Dress.

Except at low tide, when all meet, you will find each person at his own work, which is often different from that of his neighbour; for each house has to supply everything for itself as far as it can. Some villages have no *Pandanus* or pan-leaf and are supplied from others; but what they are possessed of each man must look to for himself. To get *Pandanus* is left to the women, but cocoanuts the men fetch.

At low-tide, off go all spare hands to fish, the men in small canoes, one or two in each. They spear the fish and are splendid shots and sharp-eyed. Should the tide fall after dark, so much the better they say. The fisherman then holds a torch in his hand. It consists of a dry cocoanut leaf tied at intervals. Sometimes the harbour is covered with these lights at night. The man looks for fish in all directions. In his left hand he holds the torch, in his right a light spear. Way of fishing.

On those islands where there is trade with ships the inhabitants like rice very well and are eager to exchange nuts for it. Rice, an article of trade.

Though the Nicobarese have many pigs and fowls, it would be a mistake to think that they eat much meat. On common occasions 'larome' (*Pandanus* bread), cocoanut fruit or rice is their main food, together with fish. Fish they are very eager to obtain. They fry it on a spit and eat it half-raw. Only on great occasions will they kill pigs and fowls; and then they have a regular feast, eating as much as they can, and drinking the toddy of the cocoanut-palm till they are quite drunk. Such a feast generally goes on for a day or two. Their food.

charge, mentions as the reasons why the attempt did not succeed, that it was a bad time of the year, the winds were high, the rains were washing over the land, the want of proper discipline, difference of opinion between the officers of the expedition, and consequently disorderly conduct of the men. Drink, disorderly life, unwholesome food, sleeping exposed to the night air (which even the Nicobarese took care not to do) ruined their health. Mr. Wolquarts is said to have been too sparing in care of the sick men and in refreshments for the laborers. Mr. Lund further insinuates that Mr. Wolquarts owed his death to being too liberal to himself! The sickness, however, decreased; they began cutting down jungle, to collect betel-nuts and cowries to send away in ships that were to arrive.

Then a new officer, Jens Tweed, arrived with a reinforcement of two invalids to Camorta. Governor Jens Tweed seems to have been an old man given to drink, and he died after eighteen days' residence at the Nicobars. On his voyage to Camorta (now called Nancowry) he touched at Great Nicobar, and he brought a number of the natives from this island, who however suffered from some infectious disease, and the men of the Danish Settlement caught it. Sickness increased; their courage began to fail, and the Nicobarese began to worry them. The Nicobarese who arrived with Mr. Tweed robbed the Settlement stores, and the Camorta men assisted them. They threatened fire and murder if they did not get at once the guns, powder and balls. The settlers were too few and too weak to resist; they tried to make peace and sought safety in flight, and went to Achin in Sumatra in the *Ebenezer*, which was lying in the harbour.

1768–1787. Moravian Brethren.

The Danish India Company lost, after the beforementioned unlucky attempts, all courage, and offered the Moravian Brethren privileges if they would attempt to convert the Nicobarese and to colonise the islands. Count Zinzendorff, the founder of the sect and their mission college, had a long correspondence about the matter, and the result was that the Moravian Brethren were allowed to begin a settlement at the Nicobars or elsewhere in the Danish possessions. In the year 1759 (or three years after Mr. Wolquarts took possession of Camorta) a number of Brethren arrived at Tranquebar. It may here be noticed that the first Protestant missionaries who ever came out to India came out with a view to christianise the Nicobars, and were subsidised by the Danish Government at a time when the Hon. East India Company would not allow a Christian minister of any sect within its dominions for fear that they might interfere with trade. They had, however, no means to carry out their Christian and charitable intentions, so they settled quietly at Tranquebar and bided the time when they could start. At last after eight years' expectations, in 1768, six Moravian Brethren arrived at Nancowry, accompanied by six 'Evangelists,' six European soldiers, and six sepoys. The old author from whom I am quoting is very angry with the Brethren for not fetching themselves wives from Bompoka or elsewhere. He calls it a 'He-colony.' The missionaries of this sect, who spent so many years at Nancowry harbour, did not succeed however in christianising the natives, or making a good settlement. They had to earn their bread by the sweat of their brows. Some of the most curious land-shells and sea-shells which science possesses, and which are to this day unique specimens, were collected by these noble men, who had to trade for their subsistence and to look to the seasons for their food and necessaries. It may not be wondered at that the natives were not converted; for they do not esteem a man who trades with them for his living, and could not be brought to believe that these men came to bring them light and truth.

The Moravian missionaries kept up their establishment from 1768 to 1787, or nineteen years; but as late as 1804 a man called Palmer and his wife went to this place. He also was a Moravian Brother. In 1768, when they first settled, they squatted in an open space between the villages of Malacca and Inuange. The remains of their brick-house is now inside a peepul-tree, and a brick-well is still a silent and eloquent witness of these men, whom the love of God brought from their country far away to die in His cause, and though no visible traces are to be seen in the doings or sayings of the natives, still they have not lived in vain. The example of good men may have left some good among their neighbours. An old man told me, in 1871, that his father had told him of the Europeans who lived there when he (the father) was a little boy, and he said that the spirits did them no harm while those men lived there, but when they went away, sickness took the upper hand. The bricks, which these Europeans made with their own hands a hundred years ago, are now part of the big well in the new English settlement. This was the condition attached to their permission to go to the Nicobars:—that the Moravian Brethren were bound to keep up a colony, so that the sovereignty of the Danish King might not be doubted or endangered. During their stay the Austrians made an attempt to colonise the islands, which were Danish at this time, as the following will show,—and I here add the necessary information to supply the Austrian version of the affair, which will be found in *Selections from the Records of the Government of India, Home Department*, No. LXXVII, pp. 197—203; and in the same book, pp 31—54, will be found a series of letters written in 1812 by the only surviving missionary brother Johan Gottfred Hænsel, which graphically describe the life, sufferings, and fate of these men and their mission. In the year 1784 the Danish Government sent a supply of provisions and a wooden house. Up to that year twenty-four missionaries had died,—thirteen in Nancowry and eleven shortly after their arrival at Tranquebar.

On the 6th of June 1778 arrived the Imperial Roman (*i. e.*, 1778.
Austrian) frigate *Joseph and Maria Theresa* and anchored in Austrian attempt.
Nancowry harbour by Camorta. The Commander, Captain Bennett, visited the Brethren at Nancowry and inspected their establishment; asked about the quality of the soil; what the aim of the settlers was, and informed them that the frigate carrying forty-eight guns —had left Livorno under the command of Lieutenant-Colonel von

Boltz, who now was stopping on the Malabar coast in Palampatam, from whence he had sent him to the Nicobar Islands. Captain Bennett then showed the Brethren his orders from Lieutenant-Colonel von Boltz and gave them a copy.

In this letter, Lieutenant-Colonel von Boltz, orders that, as Denmark had given up the islands, Captain Bennett was to add them to the Roman Empire. He was to visit the Moravian missionaries, take them under the protection of the Emperor, hoist the Austrian flag, and promise them good pay, as they might be useful for the trade that was to come. He was also ordered to send one of the missionaries to Lieutenant-Colonel von Boltz. The missionaries, however, according to the report, which they sent to the Danish Government, protested against these proceedings, stating that they were under the orders and protection of the Danish King and could not hoist the Imperial flag. They also refused the pay promised, and refused to come to Lieutenant-Colonel von Boltz.

Captain Bennett selected the site on which the first Danish settlement was—the very one that is now occupied by the penal settlement of the Indian Government. He began to build a house, made a garden and a road, and cut passages through the jungle. One month and six days after his arrival the ceremonies of taking possession were held. The guns were fired, and Captain Bennett proclaimed that henceforth the Nicobars belonged to the Holy Roman Empire. In August a fort was made with eight guns, and leaving three Europeans behind, the frigate sailed, never to return.

When this affair became known at Tranquebar, the Danish Government protested. Lieutenant-Colonel von Boltz excused himself, and said it was a *boná fide* transaction, as Denmark had given the islands up. He denied that the missionaries had protested, and even asserted that they consented to his taking possession. He even stated "that all the inhabitants of the four islands, "Nancowry, Camorta, Trinkut and Katchall, had with one voice "begged to be received as subjects to His Majesty the Emperor, and "under his most high protection."

This last assertion is so glaring, that I do not hesitate to state that the brave Lieutenant-Colonel must entirely have drawn on his imagination for this feeling of the natives. I can well understand that a mercantile company, as the one Colonel von Boltz served, required to put full reports from the East before the shareholders, but it is too fine to be credited by any one who has visited these islands. Von Boltz's expedition ended very soon. The three Europeans whom he left behind lived in great misery till a Danish vessel took them away to Tranquebar. The powder magazine was until lately to be seen; with it disappeared the last trace of the Austrian expedition.

1787. In the year 1787, the Moravian missionaries left the Nicobars and gave up their establishment there. The Government at Tranquebar sent over one lieutenant, a corporal and six privates to keep up the guard.

From 1787 till 1807 the Danish guard on Nancowry was kept up. 1787–1807.

In 1790, the Rev. Mr. Engelhardt was deputed by the Danish Government to report on the Nicobars and how best to make a colony. He died, however, after nineteen days' stay at Nancowry. His being sent there shows that the Danes had not given up colonising at that period. 1790: Rev. Mr. Engelhardt.

In the same year Mr. Topping, an English officer, visited the Nicobars in the cutter *Mary*. He found the guard to consist of a country-born sergeant of Dutch descent, two Mulatto soldiers, two sepoys, one artillery man and two caffree slaves.

In 1807, the English commenced war with Denmark and took possession of the Nicobars. The little guard then on the spot returned to Tranquebar. This conquest does not seem to have been recorded in history. During this period an Italian Jesuit visited Car Nicobar from Rangoon, but he had to leave the island in a short time. 1807–1814.

In 1814, the islands were given over to Denmark by the English. 1814–1831.

The Danes were thinking of colonising them, but it was not till the 1st August 1831 that a new settlement was begun under the auspices of Revd. D. Rosen. 1st August 1831. The last Danish settlement.

Mr. Rosen was a Danish Lutheran minister in Government employ at Tranquebar. He had access to the old records, and he worked himself gradually into the belief, that he could successfully colonise the Nicobars. It would of course have been a great boon to Denmark if it could have been done, as the islands are fertile, and trade might have flourished here. This could not be done at Tranquebar and Serampore, when the territory was surrounded by English land, and everything paid a transit duty of twenty per cent; so that no Danish merchant could compete with his neighbours. Mr. Rosen was enthusiastic in starting the Settlement, and hoped that it might turn out a blessing to his country, and right bravely did he try to make it succeed.

He imagined that if he should be able to surmount the difficulty of the climate, all would go well. He, for that purpose, prepared a wooden house at Tranquebar—30 feet by 12 feet and two-storied. He selected three carpenters, a cooper, a smith, a cook, twelve coolies and thirteen lascars and a European sergeant. Four cows and two bullocks were also sent.

With these men, the house and the stores, he sailed in a little schooner bought for the expedition. On the 1st August 1831 the schooner anchored in Nancowry harbour. The site selected was the same as for the first Danish settlement, where also the Austrians had been, and where now the Indian penal settlement is.

The settlers at once began making the site for a house ready. The wooden house was put up, and was inhabitable on the 10th of September. It was where the Christian prisoners' quarters are now.

Before the 1st of September half the number of the settlers were laid up with fever, and on the 11th of September the European sergeant died. He was buried below the hill, where a tree is still growing, opposite the commissariat godown. On the 22nd of September the schooner left, taking away three men that were ill. Mr. Rosen tried now to put everything in order, but he had no good food for his men, no doctor, and was obliged to practise in medicine himself. The men were dissatisfied, especially the Hindus, and the Nicobarese would not work for him. He thought the place on which they had settled was very unhealthy on account of the swamp on all sides, and made up his mind to remove to Mongkata hill further west, where the ruins are still to be seen. With much coaxing, he succeeded in getting a little of the mangrove and undergrowth cleared away, partly by the aid of the Nicobarese. As ill luck would have it, a vessel was wrecked on Little Nicobar, with two hundred natives of India on board. The Nicobarese took possession of the cargo, which consisted of cloth and tobacco, while the wrecked people came in great numbers to Mr. Rosen. The stores of the wreck spoiled the market entirely, as the natives thereby got the only luxuries they cared for, and Mr. Rosen had after that time great difficulty in procuring any supplies from them.

1st December 1831.

On the 1st December 1831 the schooner arrived again from Tranquebar. It brought a doctor, another European sergeant, some sepoys, coolies and stores. The schooner went then to Little Nicobar, and fetched the remnant of the wrecked crew up to Nancowry. Mr. Rosen could not, however, keep this number of people, especially as they would not work for their support. Nearly the whole crew was therefore shipped in the schooner for Achin on the 1st January 1832. The schooner returned on the 22nd January, but did not bring the pepper plants which Mr. Rosen so eagerly wanted, nor any hill paddy (*i. e.*, rice for seed). Mr. Rosen had up to the 16th January kept in good health, but on that day he had the first attack. Sickness increased, and the cooks were all laid up with fever. The fever never left Mr. Rosen again; till the day of his death in 1856, in Denmark, he had reminders of his stay at the Nicobars. The crops failed, and the doctor was ill.

15th April 1832. The house burnt down.

Mr. Rosen's difficulties closed in upon him from all sides. On the 15th April 1832 the schooner returned, and on the same day the wooden house was burnt with all its stores. This loss was the worst of all, for the wooden house was the best quarters in the place,—the only one which was raised from the ground. All Mr. Rosen's clothes, books, and diary were lost. This was a great misfortune; and suffering as Mr. Rosen and all his men were, he lost all faith in the two sites where they were working. He thought he would try to go to Car Nicobar with all his men.

6th July to 1st Sept. 1832. A vain attempt to visit Car Nicobar.

On the 6th July, the schooner again arrived from Tranquebar, and on the 24th Mr. Rosen shipped for Car Nicobar. The man in charge of the schooner was, however, a very bad sailor. He had no idea about reckoning, and after cruising about a good deal, they arrived on the 11th August at Djunks Island. They got water there, and left on the 22nd August. On the 1st September they returned without even having sighted Car Nicobar.

On the 8th December, Mr. Rosen went on a visit to Bompoka and Teressa to try to find a good site for a settlement, but he returned not very well pleased.

On the 9th December, the schooner arrived with orders for the return of the surgeon, and left on the 26th December.

In the beginning of 1833, one month was lost in a vain attempt to settle on Trinkut. The Nicobarese were afraid of the settlers interfering with their cocoanuts. The fever was very bad; the mosquitos, together with the sand-flies, did not allow the unfortunate settlers any sleep at night, and so the attempt was given up. 12th Jan. to 12th Feb. 1833.

On the 4th March, the schooner arrived from Tranquebar. The Danish Government was not well pleased with Mr. Rosen's plan of settling at Trinkut. 4th March. Schooner arrives.

In March the schooner started for Penang to fetch spice plants and Chinese gardeners. 18th March 1833.

The Settlement works were now progressing: salt was made; a brick-house begun, and the bricks for it partly made, partly brought from the ruins of the Moravian Brethren's house at Malacca.

In August a vessel freighted by the Tranquebar Government to bring supplies to Nancowry came in. The schooner which left on the 18th March had been unfortunate. Fever broke out among the crew. The captain and mate died; the crew deserted. The second mate attempted to bring her back, but did not succeed. He met heavy weather in the bay and had to put in to Penang. The captain of this vessel was, however, going to bring the schooner back as soon as he could. 5th August 1833.

After the vessel left, the works went on as before. Progress was made with the brick-house; sickness decreased. During the latter part of 1833 plantations were made of cocoanut trees, betel-nut, plantains, yams, mulberry, &c., &c. The burning of bricks was rather difficult, as there was no pug-mill in the Settlement. Everything seemed to thrive, when another danger appeared. On the 22nd December the supply of rice in store was only seventeen and a half bags. All supplies were nearly running out; so local industry sprang up. Mr. Rosen made his own bread; he made ghoor (*i. e.*, unrefined sugar) and salt; cocoanut oil was made for the lamps and was used instead of ghee, the supply of which had run out. On the 19th January, the rations of each man were lowered to four pounds of rice a week, and yams were substituted for the rest.

On the last day of January the schooner hove in sight, to the delight of all. She, however, only brought four Chinese gardeners and boxes with spice plants. You can imagine poor Mr. Rosen's feelings. He says that he felt like a wanderer in a desert, who, searching for water, finds gold. Spice plants he had always 31st January 1834.

imagined would be the best-paying cultivation. Now, at this moment, when they were near starvation, the gardeners and spice plants arrived. The captain who brought her down was the same man who came on the 5th of August. He found the vessel in Penang, but he suffered from fever, and when he at last started, she could not sail on account of barnacles accumulated on her. The

The schooner starts for rice.

schooner was despatched at once to Achin, but she touched the ground and could not start before the 6th of February. When she had gone, the Chinamen began to work their spice plantations, and in six weeks they were flourishing. On the 23rd of February the last rice was given out, and the settlers had only vegetables for food for some time. The men now refused to work, and Mr. Rosen was in great difficulties. He, however, made his people prepare the bread of the *Pandanus Mellori*, and before long the huts were all stocked with the *Pandanus* fruit. The health of the men was better during this period than in any previous one, but they did not work much. Mr. Rosen succeeded in getting a little rice from a Burman vessel, but only half a bag.

11th March 1834.

At last, on the 11th March, the schooner came in with rice, and the want was at an end. Now work was resumed, and half a bag of hill paddy (rice) was planted out. The Nicobarese seemed at this period a little more inclined to work on payment, and the plantations progressed well.

About this time Mr. Rosen made an excursion after the wild cattle at the north end of Nancowry. He saw their traces, but not the buffalos.

Just when everything seemed to promise success another adversity befel the unlucky Settlement. On the 4th of April the schooner was ready to start, the mails were closed, when news was brought that two Malay pirates had arrived. The Nicobarese brought news to Mr. Rosen of their movements, and as the captains of the two Malay vessels were well-known bad characters, and their behaviour was not very friendly to the natives, and as they also had made special inquiries about the Settlement, matters assumed rather a serious aspect. The schooner was detained. The lime-kiln was turned into a little fort, and wild betel-nut trees cut down and made into a stockade. The men were all armed, and strict watch was kept. As the two vessels, however, did not return from Great Nicobar, whither they had gone, and as fever broke out, the Revd. Mr. Rosen made up his mind to do without the schooner.

15th April 1834.

Two ship's guns were landed, and she started on the 15th April 1834. Mr. Rosen, after she had left, was very busy to get a place for the ammunition built inside the stockades, but in the middle of this busy time the rains broke in very violently, and the wretchedness was great. With the rains, however, the danger from the Malays ceased, for native crafts rarely beat against the monsoon. At the break of the monsoon, hill paddy was sown and throve very well. Out of half a bag, Mr. Rosen had the joy to get twelve bags. About this time the indefatigable and undaunted Mr. Rosen introduced a new sort of currency, which I cannot forbear mentioning, as it shows that the

Nicobarese are not so bad as generally believed, and that they will trust a good man's word. On arrival, tobacco leaves were found to be a good article of barter, but the tobacco had on account of the many mishaps run short, and Mr. Rosen therefore issued little slips of paper with a tobacco leaf drawn on them marked with as many dots as he promised to pay leaves. After a short while all the Nicobarese took these in payment for nuts and other things, and Mr. Rosen was able to get nuts when he wanted them. The schooner returned on 13th June with information that the Settlement was 13th June 1834. going to be broken up. Mr. Rosen was ordered to put it on a smaller scale, and to be in readiness to leave the next time the schooner arrived. As reasons for this resolution, it was stated, (*1st,*) that the Settlement did not seem to thrive, (*2nd,*) that it was too expensive, and (*3rd,*) that the climate was too unhealthy. Mr. Rosen now strove to finish the brick-house before he left; but, though the walls were put up, he never finished the roof, as both his carpenters died. A light roof of rough poles and leaves was put over.

About this time the Nicobarese asked Mr. Rosen to keep some of their children to teach them. It was, however, too late, as he was on the point of leaving. On the 1st November the schooner 1st November 1834. arrived from Tranquebar and brought a subordinate, who was to take charge of the establishment from the Revd. Mr. Rosen. The greater part of the workmen were embarked, and the Settlement may be considered as ended on the 16th December 1834, when Mr. Rosen left it, though it lingered on till 1837. Mr. Rosen had spent three and a half years in this place, and had with the means at his disposal done wonderfully well. Always active and ready for any emergency, not easily daunted, he deserves much praise, though his enterprise did not end in success. For this he was not answerable. The inadequate means at his disposal, the want of communication with his head-quarters, the paucity of his men, his want of experience, the unhealthy climate and a series of mishaps, all combined to defeat him, and he had just arrived at that point when success could have followed when he was recalled. Proper quarters were nearly finished, cultivation was flourishing, and he had learnt the language of the people of the islands. It is satisfactory to know that after his hardships in the Nicobars, he went home to Denmark, and spent his last years in a snug rectory in Zealand.

In 1845, Mr. H. Busch was sent round the Nicobar Islands in 1845. a little schooner to report on them. He was at the islands from Mr. Busch in the *L'Espiègle.* the 18th March to 19th May. His diary is found in the *Records* 18th March to 19th May 1845. *of the Government of India,* No. LXXVII, Calcutta, 1870.

In January 1846, the Danish corvette *Galatea* visited the 1846. 8th Jan. to 23rd Feb. islands. She was sent round the world on a scientific expedition The Danish by His Majesty King Christan VIII., himself a lover of art and corvette *Galatea.* a scientific man, and one of the objects of her voyage was to examine the Nicobars; and if they were thought worth colonising, she was to leave a part of her officers and crew at the islands. An old steamer, the *Ganges,* had been bought in Calcutta and placed in command of Danish officers. The expedition came

1846 to 1848 The *Ganges*. to the conclusion that an attempt at colonising the islands should be made, and the *Ganges* was left behind, when the *Galatea* proceeded, in the end of February, on her journey. The site of the Settlement was chosen on Little Nicobar in Ganges harbour, with Pulo Milo as a support.

The original journal kept on board the *Ganges*, which lies before me, illustrates, however, clearly the abortive attempt at colonising. Chinamen were imported from Penang. They cleared a little jungle; but opium was not provided, and sickness and death, as well as want of interest, made the matter drop entirely. The *Ganges* was nearly always at Penang, where it was much more agreeable to be, than at the feverish station. Then came 1848 and its political storms, and Denmark was no longer able to devote attention to these possessions. The *Galatea* and *Ganges* expeditions had cost very much money, and the best result of them was the paper written by Dr. Rink on the islands.

Dr. F. Von Hochstetter, who belonged to the *Novara* expedition, says in his own paper on the Nicobars: "As to scientific "inquiry, I left the Nicobars quite unsatisfied, in spite of the "comparatively long time of one month which we spent in their "waters. I know how little my own observations increase the "geological knowledge of these islands, for which we are indebted "to Dr. Rink; for just the grandest objects,—the Islands *Teressa*, "*Little* and *Great Nicobar*,—remain altogether a *terra incognita*."

1848: Denmark takes away her flag. In 1848, the Danish corvette *Valkyrien* was sent to take away the Dannebrog (*i. e.*, the Danish flag) from the different islands, and therewith all attempts ceased from her side.

1858: The *Novara*. On the 23rd February 1858 the Austrian frigate *Novara* anchored at Car Nicobar. She was on a scientific voyage round the world, and was especially sent to look at these islands. The report of her voyage has been printed and is well known. The commander of the expedition wrote a memorandum on the occupation of the Nicobars, and calculated the cost of the first year at £115,000.

The islands were for a long period (1848—1869) without any masters; matters were very unsatisfactory, and many complaints were made of piracies. The Indian Government then resolved on colonising them.

1869: THE ENGLISH take possession. On the 27th of March 1869 the islands were taken possession of by Commander A. Morrell of H. M. S. *Spiteful* in the name of Queen Victoria. The flag was hoisted and saluted. The proclamation was, however, found not to put the islands under the Indian Government, so the ceremony was repeated on the 16th of April 1869, and the flag was again hoisted and saluted. The Great Indian Penal Settlement at Port Blair with its inexhaustible stores and resources being the support of the new Settlement, it was an easy matter to start well. It is an easier matter, with a regular monthly steam communication, to undertake to settle in such an unhealthy place, than it was for poor Mr. Rosen with his few men, little schooner, and with Tranquebar so far off. It is no blame for the pioneers, who did not succeed in their undertaking, if the Nicobars, when taken in hand by the Indian Government and affiliated to Port Blair, will one day be an important station in the Indian seas.

H. M. S. *Dryad* came on the 24th January 1871 to Nancowry to take possession once more of the islands. She first touched at Galatea Bay in Great Nicobar, where a flag-staff was erected and the proclamation read. The site was chosen on the eastern side of the bay. The S. E. Point was called 'Hayward's Point,' the S. W. Point 'Miller's Point,' after a son of the celebrated geologist Hugh Miller, who accompanied the expedition. On the 1st of February 1871 the flag was hoisted at Car Nicobar on the eastern side of the northern bay. The bay was called 'Dryad's Bay' and the staff was erected on 'de Röepstorff's bluff' as it was called in remembrance of a Danish naval officer, who visited these islands a quarter of a century ago. This is the latest of the occasions that the islands have been taken possession of, and I hope it may be the last. 1871: The *Dryad.*

The Andamans were not permanently occupied by any European nation till the end of the 18th century. In 1789 Lieutenant Blair, acting under orders from the Hon'ble East India Company, founded a penal settlement in the great harbour on the east coast of the 'South Andaman:' this was called 'Port Cornwallis.' The place was found to be very unhealthy, and the settlement was in 1792 abandoned, and a new one opened on the 'Great Andaman.' Here also, however, sickness prevailed, and in 1793 it was given up in its turn. This second settlement was also called 'Port Cornwallis.' Andamans. Port Cornwallis. 1789—1792. New Settlement. 1792—1793.

At the close of the mutiny in 1858 the want of a penal settlement was felt, and it was decided to open out one on the site of that founded by Lieutenant Blair in 1789, and it was now called 'Port Blair.' On the 10th March 1858 the first batch of one thousand convicts, principally mutineers, arrived. Since the arrival of the first batch of convicts more than seventeen thousand have followed. Port Blair.

The Andaman Islands are densely covered with jungle, and with the exception of wild pigs, only a few berries are found in the forest to feed upon. The coast is, on the other hand, rich in shell-fish and oysters; the sea abounds in fish. The wild tribes that lived on these islands therefore kept near the sea, and not knowing the art of raising crops, lived by hunting pigs and fishing. The pigs are, however, not very plentiful, and so they mainly drew their supplies from the sea. On a convenient spot, where there was fresh water at hand, they would meet, and have their meals at these rendezvous places. A big shell-heap generally indicates where they met. These are the 'kjókkenmióddings' of these islands. If you search them, you will find that all the shells in them have been under the influence of fire; and, in such where the form makes it difficult to get the animal out, the shells have been broken, invariably on the same part. It will also be Kjókkenmióddings.

seen in searching these shell-heaps that the people have in the course of time changed their way of living. In the lower layers are found nicely-glazed pottery and iron arrow-heads.

This seems to indicate that they once were in a higher stage of civilisation than they now are. But even more peculiar is the circumstance that bones of birds are found in the lower layers, for at the time of Port Blair being opened out, they did not eat birds. Probably, with the loss of communication with the outer world and the consequent want of iron to form their arrow-heads, they gave up the chase of birds. The best eatable birds on these islands are the pigeons, but they sit high, more than one hundred feet from the ground. Oysters are found to have been the staple of their food formerly; now they will not touch them.

Origin. The Andamanese are a dwarfed, wooly-haired, dark-skinned Negrito race. I believe that they are an old people in these places. Their 'kjókkenmióddings' indicate, by their number and size, that they are either the remains of an old but not numerous people or of a numerous poople, who may have been a shorter time on these islands. And, as they were only slightly more numerous in 1792 than they are now, it is more likely that they are an old, not numerous, people. In several of the 'kjókkenmióddings' one foot or more of soil have formed above the top layer. This proves at least something.

The Revd. D. Rosen in his book on the Nicobars says that he has heard a rumour that they are the descendants of slaves wrecked on these islands. They may be; but I do not think so. They are divided into tribes, whose languages are very different, though a few fundamental words are common. This points to a length of time which has allowed the language to divide and change. Their number is, though not very great, at all events too great to suppose that they owe their origin to a few cast-away slaves. The climate is not very favorable. The Andamanese of the present day find it very difficult to rear their children. The great rains generally kill them, and it is hardly credible that the same people in a short time should have multiplied greatly and divided into tribes. I think it more likely that they are the original inhabitants of these once sterile islands, who have formerly been in a higher state of civilisation, and at all events had communication with other nations still in the stone age; for flint is found in their 'kjókkenmióddings,' and flint is not found at all *in situ* at the Andamans. They have now been trained to a certain degree and are becoming useful, bringing in runaway convicts, collecting tortoise-shells, pulling oars, and their time will soon be gone. They are passing away, as every other tribe of savages have invariably done when coming in contact with civilisation. Some of their children have been baptised, but it is an easier matter to baptise children and give them Christian names, godfathers and godmothers, than to make Christians of, and civilise the wild tribes of the jungle.

Finally, I beg to thank those officers of the Settlement who have given me assistance; also Cand. Philol. Mr. O. Siesbye, of Copenhagen, who kindly helped me with the dedication.

The copies that were printed at Port Blair having run out, the book has been reprinted at Calcutta and some remarks which I owe to the kindness of Mr. Tuson have been added.

CALCUTTA,
20th January 1875.

Vocabulary of Dialects spoken in the Nicobar and Andaman Isles.

English Words.	The Nancowry Dialect.	Great Nicobar.	Teressa by M. Plaisant.	Car Nicobar.	Inland Race 'Shobængs.'	Andaman Words.	Remarks.
A.							
Abdomen	tamhæ.						
Abhor	hat sho	...	hoh' hangatsike	at hō	gna hōā.		
Abide	katoev	ōm	...	afē-eda	katjōm.		
				ōraaka.			
Able	le-ap	leap mahoel	(*able to*) raâtk ... raâtk ane; liap.	salaura.			
Abode	gñi	gñi	...	pat-ti	nōp.		
Abominable	hat lapoé	na-koe-toe	...	o-lā-je	opō.		
Abort	...	...	kahia.				
Abortion	waing-a-jen.						
Above	lako-é-én.						
Absent	hat-ot	gna-ōt kajol	hāt; hâat	dāvakehoetnere	lāk; ohōi.		
Abstain (1)	(1) tjit	idé po	...	at kaoet	gñip.		
Abundance	ta-kadu; uróhotshe	pitō menō	hehōr karhû	marōñg	fot a goet.		
Abuse	...	...	holhœhang'en	...	...	Arb-tor-jor-kay.	
Accompany	tju dal paju	...	hehang, huleang.				
According	...	...	(*a-to*) hata. vetseng; hehōt.				
Accustom	...	...	ntsie-hœn; tsie hœn.				
Ache	tjak; tjok	tjoé	...	tjok	kái.		
Acid	ba-grein	ahoel	kâat; kâag'n	...	teit.		
Acquaint	oljol.						
Across	...	...	akhâte.				
Active	...	...	lhohatse; l'hohātse.				
Adieu (2, 3, 4)	(2) tavatse de me de roe	(2, 3, 4) tjū	...	gñei ma mœ.			
	(3) jutju	...	...	kerangnere.			
	(4) bé-haré.						
Admirable	...	...	lhâak.				

Adopted child ...	... ...	... ...	khuan-kamūin.			
Adore ...	ghen-iwi ...	... ...	... ...	... ...	ba-iwi tamnjet-jau.	
Adze ...	danăn ...	danā ...	.. ..	danan.		
Afraid ...	poho-a ... watme pohoa (*be not a*—).	ba-oe-a ...	... ...	om pahāekoe ...	toak jau (*be not a-*)	ar'h-lart-kay.
After (5) ...	(5) latdok ...	... ...	hēñ ...	... ...	kain-gné.	
Afternoon (6) ...	(6) tjin-fá-e-thé (*early part*) la-dí-e-je (*latter part*)	ka-en-te-tju (*early part*) wé-uñg (*latter part*)	... ...	sarœ heng (*early part*) perūé (*latter part*).	tju kain.	
Afterwards ...	ma kā (*in the same day*)	māo ...	... ...	talōk ...	gñé.	
Age ...	... ...	... ...	karhé pâhé. (i. e., *man's quantity*).			
Aged ...	pomoæshæ ...	omshó-ong ...	... ...	mā ...	haké jo poe.	
Agony ...	(*vide* Ache) ...					
Agreeable ...	... ...	... ...	lhâak.			
Agree ...	... ...	... ...	hehōt vetsen			
Ague ...	tō-o ...	fuok ; tō-o ...	... ...	ō-é ...	jā.	
Aim ...	harælé ...	haræle ...	akhit ...	haroelle ...	ho-e-fōñg.	
Air ...	haó ...	aha-oel ...	(*to a-*)vi khink-ha-heng ; hohæng		gūja-tji-tæ.	
Alas ...	wé-é- é.					
Alike ...	shom					
Alive ...	ye-erm (*A. C. M.*)					
All ...	omtōm ...	læt-te-ré ...	... ...	ma-laung-ge ...	goet ...	arthoo'roo-da.
Alliance ...	... ...	... ...	hahe.			
Allied ...	.. ..	... ...	hahē tin pâjé.			
Alligator ...	jé-av ...	ko-auñg ...	... ...	ko-óv.		
Allow ...	tjōk (*very long sound*).					

The vowels are sounded as in German or Hindustani ; *j* as *y* in 'yard ;' *ei* and *ai* are sounded like 'eye ;' *au* as in 'Auge' (German) ; *æ* as *ai* in 'fair ;' *œ* as in 'Oel' (German) ; *ch* soft as *ch* in 'loch.'

1.—*When in mourning or during pregnancy.*
2-3.—*The departing.* 4.—*So says the host.*

5.—*Thus E. H. M.*
6.—*E. H. M.* 1 p. m. '*tchinfoitua ;*' 3 p. m. '*tchinfoitua anhsheh ;*' 5 p. m. '*ladeya.*'

English Words.	The Nancowry Dialect.	Great Nicobar.	Teressa by M. Plaisant.	Car Nicobar.	Inland Race 'Shorængs.'	Andaman words.	Remarks.
Alone ...	heang.						
Along ...	... ...	... ...	alôhie.				
Also ...	... ...	... ...	pu.				
Always (7) ...	(7) panōne ...						
Ambergris ...	kampæ ...	kanpæ ...	kinpev; kanpà-aeh				
Ambition ...	... ...	... ...	hehomang-ta-karhū.				
Amiable ...	... ...	... ...	habé tin pâjé. (*vide* Allied).				
Amuse ...	... ...	... ...	(*a-oneself* huhi-aœt.				
Ancestor ...	... ...	... ...	ahūhot hahnhaāt.				
Anchor ...	shinpōje ...	le-shapō-i ...	sanam kaveang' nfi sanumptē.	shanuñgge.			
Anchor rope ...	... ...	... ...	pürhon-ta-karhû. kâmapê-ta-karhû.				
Anchorage ...	... ...	... ...	khiuk-khiong.				
Anger ...	... ...	... ...	(*burst of a-*) khi-ank-fo-naat. menam.				
Angry ...	mon-hang-kō ...	ka'édé ...	... ...	léu.			
Animal ...	ahéol ...	... ...	(*little a——, shell-fish*).				
	(*little a——, shell-fish*).	... ...	enrhui. (*not man*) hat-pahé.				
Ankle ...	oglá galá ...	eloe-galá ..	... ...	oglaé.			
Anna ...	(8-*anna piece*) Rupia dit malau. (4-*anna piece*) Rupia olmat itjé. (2-*anna piece*) Rupia ishakā.						

Annihilate ...	... ...	... ...	vi-hat.			
Announce ...	... ...	... ...	nghēn.			
Annoyance ...	... ...	... ...	kistot.			
Annual ...	som en ju (*half-yearly*)	tjom-en-bihé ...	... ...	saróg̃ne.		
Another ...	dev-ve ... (*another time*) se-ju	dev ... (*another time*).	(*one another*) kua.			
	another man) pa-ju dev-ve.	sáoév	ki, kaa.			
Answer (8) ...	ōpshāp ...	jŭ-a ...	schap ...	(8) shop loa tju.		
Ant ...	midorā ...	... ...	telȧat. ...	... .	... ...	am-ma-da.
Antler (9) ...	hintōp ...	... ...	(9) ntâak.			
Anvil ...	... ...	... ...	anet.			
Anxious ...	... ...	... ...	kistot.			
Ape (10) 11 ...	(10) kéin, doœng	pajun ...	kaiing, kejin.			
Appetite (12) ...	oi-g̃na ...	pató-ang ...	honhe ...	(12) tjomhæ ..	go-it.	
Approach ...	... ...	... ...	hēm.			
Approval ...	... ...	... ...	hehot-vetsen.			
Arbitrator ...	... ...	... ...	pâhé-ta-ghēn. (*i. e., man who speaks*)			
Areca-nut (13) (14)	(13) hija ...	omtjong ...	(14) ...	tisa-ak ...	en-tjo-ong.	
Arise ...	tjé-a-ka ...	... ...	... ...	... ...	... ...	bo-e-kay.
Arm (15) ...	(15) koal ...	koal ...	khor kél ; mhakti	kel ...		
Armpit ...	ol-o-do-á.					
Arrack ...	wiinje ; terum ...	terum ...	tarām ...	terum ...		la-ha-e.
Arrive ...	... ...	... ...	reugk ; theûn.			

The vowels are sounded as in German or Hindustani; *j* as *y* in 'yard;' *ei* and *ai* are sounded like 'eye;' *au* as in 'Auge' (German); *æ* as ai in 'fair;' *œ* as in 'Oel' (German); *ch* soft, as *ch* in 'loch.'

7.—*E. H. M. has 'dul:' it seems doubtful, as the natives do not recognise it.*
8.—*G. 'Oljoala.'*
9.—*Danish 'Tak.'*
10.—*Novara. 'Dooaeen kaeen.'*
11.—*Kalchall Island. deRff. 'morang-she.'*
12.—*G. 'Thaap,' doubtful.*
13.—*G. 'Nhjă,' 'enau.' The natives do not recognise the latter.*
14.—*deRff. 'Hinang.'*
15.—*E. H. M. 'chee-koal,' not recognised.*

English Words.	The Nancowry Dialect.	Great Nicobar.	Teressa by M. Plaisant.	Car Nicobar.	Inland race 'Shobængs.'	Andaman words.	Remarks.
Arrow	bel	eufæhnje	... ...	endreien	... ...	(*for fish*) rā-ta. (*for pigs*) i-a-la-da.	
Arrowroot	amæ.						
Art	... ...	... ...	ta-liap.				
Article (of speech)	te-	... ...	ta-				
As	... ...	... ...	tsic; iana; ianet.				
Ascend	... ...	... ...	hole.				
Ashes	ben ho-ā-we	fung; ben-ho-ā-we	... ...	sitōm			
Ask (16)	(16) hamā	... ...	hahē	haró-ang	goe nang-a	e-ché-we-rar-kay	
Asleep	ithēak	koming	... ...	lōm	gño-in.		
Assist (17)	loa	... ...	l'hōrnang.				
Assure	... ...	... ...	rhaâtk-ghēn.				
Asterides	hatein paja.						
Attend on	... ...	... ...	huleang.				
Attention	... ...	... ...	kom ta akah.				
Avarice	ho-o-en-tjua.						
Augment	... ...	... ...	hēhănē.				
Avidity	... ...	... ...	hehomang-ta-karhû.				
Aunt	hotjié	omt-jokô	... ...	jung-tju	dôi.		
Authorize	... ...	... ...	along.				
Await	pænterējen; ka-toev	péteréet meōm	nphê	dahāiteren	dæ-æterekoen.		
Away	... ...	... ...	(*take a-*) hæle.				
Axe	enloin	ngūm	hamang	hanēang	karon		
Azure	tjumóa	tjong-ma.					
B.							
Baby	enmāne; kanjom tompænshe	mjé ta de eñg	... ...	gñia de kontæno	koe-et-ta-tje-en.		
Bachelor	iloō	ba-rō-e-ka	... ...	hat pehov	ba-gna-le	argó-carda-carda	

Back (18) (19) ...	(19) ōk ; la ōk ...	tabakut ; ko ...	la-huk ...	18 ok ...	tamnōi ...	oth-goó-thor-da-
Backside ...	G. tam.					
Backbone ...	hankōe.					
Bad (20) (20A) ...	(20) hat lapoé ...	... ...	... ...	hat lak ...	... ...	jabagda. arb-jar-bug-da. 20 A.
Bag ...	shajor.					
Balance ...	... ...	... ...	te-nam.			
Bald ...	gna-koi ...	hé-koi ...	... ...	gñā-koi.		
Ball ...	ahēol ...	... ...	pale.			
Bamboo (21) (22)	(22) hetwa ...	ho-o-e ...	hahaā ...	(21) hao.		
	(*cask of b-*) { kanhām	... ...	... ...	*cask of b-* } (22) tjanæ-ta.		
	{ karoeka	... ...	... ...			
	(*bamboo posts outside villages*) } kaneie	kaneie ...	... ...	*bamboo posts outside village* } mai-e.		
Banana ...	hibū ...	shōāt ...	... ...	ta-jung-gñe ...	mum.	
Bandage ...	dūne ...	... ...	... ...	laéen.		
Banner ...	hinwæ.					
Barber ...	paju kohā koi ...	hohēnne ...	... ...	kohāke.		
Bark ...	loa ...	... ...	nko.			
Barrel ...	pipe ...	pafunte ...	... ...	pep.		
Barren ...	hat kōnje.					
Basin ...	shok shanei tai... (*i. e. wash hands*)	... ...	... ...	... ...	hoshætewei.	
Basket ...	kanhong (*for catching fish*)	inōla ...	... ...	kovaake (*for catching fish*)	kantjema.	
	kanshōla (*for fowls*)	hintain ...	ntanhje ...	kanshōla (*for fowls*).		

The vowels are sounded as in German or Hindustani; *j* as *y* in 'yard;' *ei* and *ai* are sounded like 'eye;' *au* as in 'Auge' (German); ae as *ai* in 'fair;' *œ* as in 'Oel' (German); *ch* soft as *ch* in 'loch.'

16.—*E. H. M.* '*atot.*'
17.—*Schowra Island, deRff.* '*lornang.*'
18.—*deRff.* '*kiwel;*' *doubtful.*
19.—*E. H. M.* '*oke.*'
20.—*E. H. Man,* '*menkainy asheh;*' *surely a mistake!*
20*A*.—*Little Andaman, deRff,* '*makóng bata.*'
21.—*G.* '*has.*'
22.—*G.* '*djugar.*'

English Words.	The Nancowry Dialect.	Great Nicobar.	Teressa by M. Plaisant.	Car Nicobar.	Inland Race 'Shobængs.'	Andaman Words.	Remarks.
	tjukæ æ (*close-grained, little*). hintain (*close, big*)	... ...	... ...	hāat (*close-grained, little.*)			
Bast ...	akhau (*peculiar cloth made of the Sestus tree. At the Great Nicobars it was before used as clothing*)	... ...	datjaagela (*wreath of b-*)	... ...	kŏ-wī (*Sestus bark*).		
Bat ...	manlehj-ne. mognéak (*flying fox*)	ko-leigña (*fly foz*)					
Bathe (23) ...	(23) joko-leit ...	koleit ... lamoeang.	hatielk; hatiel-mang hadju; to-hiæke-te.	hau-wōk ...	hŏhōm ...	lood-gar-kay.	
Bay ...	... ...	... ...	laksi kaiit. khui-men.				
Be ...	ôt ...	... ...	... ...	... ...	... ...	mieh-e-bar-da. (*what is it*). millokay (*be quiet*).	
Beach ...	tjaka já je.						
Bead (24) ...	malau (*glass beads.*)	malau ...	... ...	tahóata ...	hóe shin lau-e...	chel'-lim-da.	
Beak ...	gmoa ...	motjé ...	... ...	almaé.			
Beard (25 26) ...	(25) nhoing ...	kanonp ...	nmanhje ...	main-ko-a.			
Beat ...	ori, fæhnwe ... (rukal, olkul)	fó-ong ...	fhâ̤â, hilee ...	faéle ...	hæn-ei ...	oth-pár-ra-kar. the-kay.	
Beautiful ...	lapoa ...	kō-e-tō ...	... ...	... ...	kōe-to.		
Because ...	... ...	... ...	katsi.				
Become ...	iwi ...	... ...	ivi.				
Bed ...	hilaôk ...	hiloe-e ...	... ...	tjamam.			
Bee ...	sæ-ho-lōw-we ...	toñg-gña- ...	... ...	... ...	holoeñg-wa ...	booth-ma-da.	
Beetle ...	met-jat-jok.						

Before (27) ...	27 d a l e i-k a-h æ (*not behind*) tiram (*in time*).	endāp (*in time*)...	huheñ ...	gnei tjua masi—(*in time*)	poël.	
Begin (28) ...	(28) wē ...	... ...	hanhangta.			
Beginning ...	... ...	... ...	hanhangta-næt.			
Behind ...	ta-la-auk ...	tomnoi ...	huk-hogn ...	la-auk.		
Belch ...	ho-ov ...	o-koe ...	... ...	ko-ov-ve ...	o-ōel.	
Bell ...	tinkæng ...	... ...	uschthân ...		... ...	wo-be-tar-da.
Belly (29) ...	wiang ...	... ...	viam ...	29 aithje ...	i-up ...	arb-jo-do-da.
Below ...	(*E. H. M.*) deg...	... ...	... ...		kau.	
Belt ...	næt on júang ...	kat-ta-kawoek ...	... ...	janèt rat.		
Bemoan ...	tjīm ...	pareit ...	... ...	pe-in ...	... ...	te-gi-ke.
Bend ...	dohn ...	lōma ...	... ...	drōne.		
Beneath ...	(*E. H. M.*) hakté.					
Betel (30, 31, 32) ...	(*b-nut*) hija ...	(*b-nut*) umtjum...	(*b-nut*) hehjā	(*b-nut*) tisar.		
	(30) (*b-nut tree*) o-gñi-ha-hija.	... ...	... ...			
	(*do. wild*) uloga hija.	(*wild b-nut tree*) kana-gñæ.	... ...	(*wild b-nut tree*) malau-gñe.		
	(*b-crusher*) lano hija.	... ...	... ...	(*b-crusher*) sanoñg.		
	(*b-box*) tan-āp ...	... ...	... ...	(*b-box*) nañg-pe.		
	(*b-bark*) h i l ó a hija.	... ...	... ...			
	(31) (*b-leaf*) akæ	(*b-leaf*) panong...	... ...	(*b-leaf*) takei-tje.		
	(*wild b-leaf*) akæ ká.	... ...	... ...	(*wild b-leaf*) kahe takei-tje.		
				(*imported do*) tao-in takei-tje.		
Better ...	... ...	... ...	hehaué-lopæh ... (*tob-*)hehăué-lopat iwi hoatse.			

The vowels are sounded as in German or Hindustani; *j* as *y* in 'yard;' *ei* and *ai* are sounded like 'eye;' *au* as in 'Auge' (German); ae as *ai* in 'fair;' *œ* as 'Oel' (German); *ch* soft as *ch* in 'loch.'

23.—*G.* '*jojoleit;*' *E. H.* '*Man lown?;*' *not recognised by the natives.*
24.—*deRff. Schowra Island* '*hijok.*'
25.—*Barbe has* '*boyalkiah*' *obsolete.*
26.—*deRff. Schowra Island* '*enkein.*'
27.—*E. H. M.* '*hadek.*'
28.—*E. H. M.* '*hoolatai*' *doubtful.*
29.—*G.* '*aithii.*'
30.—*E. H. Man,* '*tcheea heeya?*'
31.—*E. H. Man* '*dai-heeya?*'
32.—*deRff;* '*betel-leaf,*' *Schowra Island,* '*hiju.*'

English Words.	The Nancowry Dialect.	Great Nicobar.	Teressa by M. Plaisant.	Car Nicobar.	Inland race 'Shobængs.'	Andaman Words.	Remarks.
Beverage ...	... ...	... ...	kanhiong.				
Big (33) ...	(33) kadū ...	omtein tu ...	... ...	po-eje ...	hoe-bashoeit goet.		
Bill ...	gmoá (*i. e., beak*)						
Bird (34) (35) (36)	(34) sitjóā ...	... ...	sikiâ ...	(35) tjæhe-tjon...	(36) sæ-tjo-a...	choó-la.	
Birds-nest (37 (38) (39).	(37) 38 (*any b-*) hatleit (*edible*) hikāē.	a-i ...	khæt ...	kæ ...	... ...	ar-bar-rar-tar-da.	
Biscuit (40) (41)	(40) poáng ...	... ...	... ...	(41) biskot.			
Bite (42) ...	(42) ôpkăp ...	... ...	fuat ...	hokâp ...	kenjt po ...	chor-pé-kay.	
Bitter (43) ...	tæăk ...	... ...	43 hat-tsiang ...	konjā ...	paka.		
Bivalve ...	hagña-ó.						
Black (44) ...	(44) oel ...	... ...	hehu; hifu-mæt hifu-heu ... (*make bl-*) athuak	toring ...	metj ...	wo-lu-bai-a-da.	
Blacksmith ...	dom ...	toe-a.					
Bladder ...	katlaut ...	... ...	hanang.				
Blade ...	(*bl-of sword*) in-oat-te kaling. (*i. e., foreigner's knife*).						
Blind (45) (46) ...	(45) hat-hew ...	gna puje ve tō ...	hathahea ... 46 (*bl-on one eye*) imiang-ti-emat	at moek ...	... ...	e-tar-par-do.	
Block ...	oróhăka (*of a ship*).						
Blockade (47) ...	... ...	... ...	47 pamoiñ.				
Blood (48) (48A)	wāh. (*F. E. T.*) ou-al-koi (??) 48A.	... ...	... ...	(48) maham ...	tjé-tjéng ...	ārb-theé-da.	
Blow ...	hehei (*bl-the nose*)	... ...	(*to b-*) nfâa ...	kofat ...	... ...	(*to bl-*) ar-kun-gir-re-mar-kay. (*it bl-s hard*) wool-lun-tho-gada.	
Blue (49) ...	49 tjumóa (*F. E. T.*) tjong.	tjong-ma ...	nâale.				

Board ...	... ...	... ...	(*go on b-*) hafot sang'n.			
Boat (50) (51) ...	50 dué (*Nicobar canoe*). hinfoal (*Burmese canoe*). hifue (*European boat*).	doe (*canoe*)	... ...	ab (*canoe*) ... hifúe } batel } (*European boat*).	kehā (*canoe*) ...	ba-ja-da.
Body ...	(*Novara*) okaha	hóha ...	hæn'he ...	... ...	... ...	arb-chow-da.
Boil ...	(*to b-*) koholæ ...	en póe ...	(*to b-*) kaâal ... (*a b-*) ntsang; hifu.	karijé.		
Bone ...	oñg-eñg ...	in eñg ...	kolrān khium-neng. ...	... ...	ka-a-eng ...	tár da.
Book ...	lepré ...	... ...	... ...	kotje lépré.		
Boot (52) ...	52 shupāta ...	... ...	... ...	enjul kuntran.		
Borrow ...	... ...	... ...	metām.			
Bosom ...	ol-endaie ...	peteigñe ...	... ...	el gñok.		
Bottle (53) ...	(53) pentañgniñg	eeboo (*wicks*) ...	... ...	pillon.		
Bough ...	... ...	... ...	(*flower b-*) eang-ta schiâ.			
Boundary ...	... ...	... ...	mang.			
Bow (54) (55) (56)	(54) (55) foing ...	... ...	... ...	lindrijen ...	foing ...	karma.
Bow (*of a ship*) ...	shin-gol-shé-dé...	... ...	(*b-net*) karûije.			

The vowels are sounded as in German or Hindustani; *j* as *y* in 'yard;' *ei* and *ai* are sounded like 'eye;' *au* as in 'Auge' (German); *ae* as *ai* in 'fair;' *œ* as in Oel' (German); *ch* soft as *ch* in 'loch.'

33.—*A. C. Man 'karup.'*
34.—*'Novara sichna,' perhaps from Teressa?*
35.—*Galathea, 'mischiana?'*
36.—*Doubtful.*
37.—*Fontana, 'inlegne,' obsolete!*
38.—*E. H. Man 'honkang,' not recognizable.*
39.—*deRff. Schowra and Bompoka (eatable b-) 'ka.'*
40.—*Malay.*
41.—*Portuguese.*
42.—*Notice the difference in pronunciation from 'tortoise-shell.'*
43.—*Means 'not sweet.'*
44.—*Fontana, 'thanula,' obsolete!*
45.—*E. H. Man, 'pukeean.'*
46.—*Would in Nancowry dialect sound 'ho-méang-te olmat;' means 'one eye.'*
47.—*Means 'fight.'*
48.—*Galathea has 'mam.' (F E. T. stands for Tuson.)*
48A.—*I have entered Mr. Tuson's word; it means 'blood on the head.'*
49.—*Galathea 'aul' means 'black.'*
50.—*Hœnsel 'palong,' obsolete!*
51.—*'Pateal,' (deRff.,) Schowra Island, 'European boat.'*
52.—*E. H. Man has 'denapla' means 'stockings.'*
53.—*Galathea has 'hanaschalei,' very doubtful.*
54.—*'fun' (Teor) Wallace, 'fean' (Mysol) idem.*
55.—*Novara, 'donna?'*
56.—*de Rff., Schowra 'lindreijen.'*

English Words.	The Nancowry Dialect.	Great Nicobar.	Teressa by M. Plaisant.	Car Nicobar.	Inland race 'Shobængs.'	Andaman Words.	Remarks.
Box (57) ...	hoptæp (*b-of wood*)	... ...	setum ...	kāpa (*b-of wood*).			
	tanâp (*betel b-*)...	... ...	hātep ...	tasille (*b-of bark*).			
	tafôl } (*b-of bark* tashule } *of trees*)	}	57 kasson.				
Boy (58) ...	(58) kanjom ...	... ...	khiniong ... nkonje.	gnie ...	... ...	ub'boola.	
Braces (*of trowsers*)	kinshoá kanhá ...	... ...	... ...	tjanha moetá.			
Bracelet ...	(*b-for the arm*) hadlôt. (*b-for the leg*) hin-kāp-la.	... ...	atlhāāt ...	lôt (*for arm or leg*).			
Brain ...	kandoin ...	kei-peiñg ...	akotpo-ite ...	kalpeit o koi.			
Brass ...	(*Novara*) kalahaee.						
Brave ...	(*E. H. Man*) yoc-kohaká.	... ...	... ...	... ...	... ...	ar-lar'-ty-yar'-bar.	
Bread (59) (60) (61)	(59) poang. (60) rôti. (61) larôme ...	pué (61).	... ...	(61) ko-æi.			
Break ...	dæchna ...	ko-ách-gna-to ...	heâgn (*hægn*) (*br-up*). huh'hægn (*do.*) pataxi; ràkn.	ochne ...	... ...	coô-joo-ree-kay.	
Breast (62) (63) (64)	(62) olendaie ... (63) toā.	(62) peteigñe ...	... ...	62 elgnôk.			
	(64) ta ...	... ...	... ...	64 tæ.			
Breath ...	hoeng ...	... ...	... ...	ohāp.			
Breathe ...	tan-ejūm ...	hóv-va ...	... ...	hehum.			
Brecches ...	kanha ...	... ...	... ...	kinha.			
Brilliant ...	... ...	... ...	mâke.				
Briug ...	okæ; halœ ...	... ...	hukét, hukiét ...	kæ-a ...	... ...	ormokay.	
	halea; kataé (*F. E. T.*) eeneen.	... ...	kom-ta-liap (*b-knowledge*).	lo-ka ...	... ...	ekay.	

Brinjal (*solanum melongena*).	kéal ...	... ...	... ...	roñgkéal.			
Broken ...	(*vide* Break) ...	... ...	... ...	ochna ...	lita.		
Broom ...	efa ol gñi ...	... ...	... ...	fóa ...	mo-i dæt.		
Brother (65) (66)	(65) (*young br-*) tau	... ...	eo nang ...	(*young br-*) kaham	(*young br-*) pau.		
	66 (*elder br-*) tjau	... ...	... ...	(*elder br-*) mæm	(*elder br-*) hō-she.		
Brother-in-law	ha-e-i ...	... ...	hahie ...	ha-é ...	tō-o.		
Brow ...	(*eye br-*) pujol aukmat.	pehol olmat ...	... ...	shanói ma.			
Brown ...	perang ? ...	... ...	sakiāh.		ledo.		
Bruise ...	... ...	... ...	... ...	... ...	kanoi.		
Brush ...	kota koi shanôt. fanakoi. ...	... ...	(*to br-*) sum ...	kanôt ...			
Bucket (67) (68)	(67) lā pipa ...	... ...	... ...	68 balti.			
Bud ...	shi-o-un ...	... ...	kana-khiâ. kinlap-kinlôh.				
Buffalo ...	kapo ; kuban ? ...	... ...	krebō.				
Bug ...	he-oel.						
Building ...	kiong-kaling ...	... ...	... ...	... ...	pa-ko-a-me.		
Bullet (69) ...	(69) aheól ...	... ...	... ...	... ...	fung.		
Burial ...	ol ōle ...	ehōje ...	... ...	oplabo.			
Burn ...	... ...	... ...	(*to b-*) athuāk nghong. ...	... ...	... ...	chápa-in-olun-ga-kæ.	
Bury ...	ol ōle ...	... ...	hotsiét pâhé-ka. mapet (*i. e., sink dead man*).				

The vowels are sounded as in German or Hindustani; *j* as *y* in 'yard;' *ei* and *ai* are sounded like 'eye;' *au* as in 'Auge' (German); *æ* as *ai* in 'fair;' *œ* as in 'Oel' (German; *ch* soft as *ch* in 'loch.'

57.—*French.*
58.—*E. H. Man has 'lit'; not correct.*
59 *and* 60.—*from the Malay.*
61.—*of the Pandanus fruit.*
62.—*chest.*
63.—*breasts (woman).*
64.—*b-nipple.*

65.—*Novara 'tschao-anyana' probably for 'sister.'*
66.—*E. H. M. 'tchao-enlooya' (own br-)?*
'tama oosheh' (half br-)?
'tchao' (abstract brother)? (sic!)
67.—*Portuguese.*
68.—*Hindustani.*
69.—*E. H. Man, 'plooroo!'*

English Words.	The Nancowry dialect.	Great Nicobar.	Teressa by M. Plaisant.	Car Nicobar.	Inland race 'Shobængs.'	Andaman Words.	Remarks.
Burst (*of anger*) ...	mong-hang-ko ...	... ...	kiank-fô-nâat ...	... ...	gñi-ohoei.		
Bush ...	... ...	... ...	khiâ-te-pemet. scheu (*i. e., little tree*).				
Business ...	... ...	... ...	kunvi kunhuhomi kuntot.				
Butterfly ...	kalo gñave.						
Button (70) ...	(70) kantjap.						
Buy (71) ...	(71) balau ...	... ...	... ...	hau-wah-he ...	hoë fæam.		
By ...	me-æ-ho (*near by*).	... ...	ta-nhjēē } (*near by*).				
By-and-bye (71A)	(*F. E. T.*) mackei (71A).		hemæn }				
C.							
Cable ...	nut shinpojeja.						
Cage ...	gñi holpōl ...	... ...	khiuk-sikiâ ... (*i. e., place for birds*).	... ...	bashoei.		
Cake ...	hom lem.						
Calculate ...	harrow ...	... ...	harâak.				
Calf (*of the leg*) ...	kanmoana ...	kanmoana ...	... ...	... ...	... ...	arb-tár-da.	
Call ...	o-tji-o-a ...	... ...	hahem ...	... ...	mænde (*i. e., what is it called*).	arbó-mokay.	
Calm ...	gñam ...	lat-ji-akla ...	hukèt vim (*invite*)				
Camp ...	... ...	... ...	... ... khiuk-pamoni (*i.e., place for war*).	... ...	shoæng.		
Cancer ...	tang.						
Cannibal ...	(*Fontana*, 1778) gomoi.						
Candle ...	manja ...	enhéang.					
Candlestick ...	la-manjá ...	... ...	l'hæt-tamsí				
Cane ...	nāt.						

Cannon ...	hinkok.					
Cannonball ...	... ...	... ...	pâlé-ta karhû (*big ball*).			
Canoe ...	(*Nicobar c*-)dué...	doe	rae ...	(*Hamilton*, 1801) app.	(*Nicobar c*-) ho kehas.	ba-ja-da.
	(*Burmese c*-) hin-foat.	... ...	... ...	... ...	(*Burmese c*-) pine.	
Canvass ...	loé kanama.					
Cap ...	lom-teint ; kere-busse.					
	(*c-of gun*) kanap-hin-dæl (*i. e., gun's tooth*).					
Captain ...	(*chief*) omiá ...	... ...	kaptan ...	... ...	kom shoñg ve.	
	captan ...	... ...	nmbænhje (*old*)			
Cargo ...	ōk jūk ...	... ...	harâak kioug			
Carpenter ...	mamaong ...	... ...	tukan-kaim.			
Carve ...	olekal.					
Cash (72) ...	(72) (*copper money*) Sancta Maria.					
Cask (73) ...	(73) pipa ...	... ...	pipa ...	... ...	pafūnte.	
Cat (74) ...	(74) kotjing ...	... ...	meang ...	... ...	tjing ...	by'-arn-da.
Catch ...	ōk-shūp ...	pata chohu ...	... ...	... ...	... ...	ai-ne-kay.
	(*when falling*) lé	... ...	... ...	... ...	... ...	(*c.-turtle*) yar thé thood-kay.
						(*c-fish*) yarth-da-taj-kay.
Cause ...	... ...	... ...	nheōle-vite.			
Cave ...	o-how-æ ...	a-i ...	khiuk titial (*i. e., dark place*).			
Cease ...	(*imperative*) léat	let ...	ntâ ...	... ...	ohoei.	

The vowels are sounded as in German or Hindustani; *j* as *y* in 'yard;' *ei* and *ai* are sounded like 'eye;' *au* as in 'Auge' (German); *æ* as *ai* in 'fair;' *œ* as in 'Oel' (German); *ch* soft as *ch* in 'loch.'

70.—*Gal. 'enmogne-kniniut?' The latter half means 'coat.' The first half is doubtful.*

71.—*Fontana* 1795 *has 'hacaou,' evidently the same word.*

71*A*.—*Vide* 'Afterwards.'

72.—*A curious trace from the time when the Portuguese traders were common in the Indian seas! At present the pice are honored with this name.*

73.—*Portuguese.*

74.—*A Malay word which was in* 1778 *and is still in use.*

English Words.	The Nancowry Dialect.	Great Nicobar.	Teressa by M. Plaisant.	Car Nicobar.	Inland race 'Shobængs.'	Andaman Words.	Remarks.
Centipede ...	(*little c-*) tjunkoi	kave tjondeka-æ-ap.	... ...	... ...	pamain ...	kar'-rup-thar-da.	
	(*big c-*) ka-æ-ap.						
Cerute ...	unhoin honlam	hilūc ...	... ...	... ...	pania.		
Chætodon ...	meh ængje.						
Chain (75) ...	(75) (*of silver*) shahijôk.	tehija.					
		thija.					
Chair ...	katæ-dæ.						
	enpōje.						
Chalk ...	shun ...	... ...	lanet ...	... ...	kabev.		
Change ...	(*i. e., barter*) bar-row.	... ...	(*to ch-*) hahehôk.				
Channel ...	... ...	... ...	taring.				
Character ...	... ...	... ...	kalhjåat.				
Charcoal ...	shom joang ...	shâk ...	... ...	... ...	shâk.		
Chastity ...	... ...	... ...	tschu-khugtôt.				
Cheap (76) ...	(76) ta pua ...	... ...	hat tôt ...	... ...	gna-tôt.		
Cheat (77) ...	mitai ...	... ...	mitaö ...	... ...	omjokka.		
	(77) kalo ...	... ...	âlam ...	... ...	balai.		
Cheek (78) ...	tapoá ...	noïn ...	... ...	tapoa ...	gnoa-tjie ...	e-garb-da. goobda. (*O.H.B.*)	
Chest (*box*) (79) ...	(79) hoptæp ...	... ...	... ...	... ...	lafol.		
Chest (*breast*) (80)	olendêie ...	na ...	... ...	... ...	næ itenje ...	oth-coog'-da.	
Chew ...	ol-lofong.						
Chicken ...	koen-kamóe ...	... ...	(*gon haiom*) khuan kamuin.	... ...	tjóang ogнoak.		
Chief ...	omja ...	... ...	khui-kaptan ...	... ...	omibatei aoi.		
Child ...	kanjom ...	... ...	khinione ...	(*Galatea*) nhja	kœ-e ...	ob-ló-gar-da. biōla. (*O.H.B.*)(*child-birth*) adaleeka. (*O. H. B.*) (*be with ch-*) ar-boodeeda	
	kon-tje ...	... ...	khuan ...	(*Hamilton*, 1801) chu.	... ...		

Chilli (*capsicum*)	koméante ...	... ...	... ...	... ...	kóa.	
Chin ...	enkoin ...	... ...	... ...	... ...	mjen te tjean...	ar-kar-thar'-da.
Churchyard ...	... ...	... ...	(*place for ghosts*) khiuk hivi.			
Cicada ...	koloriw ...	... ...	... ...	... ...	wéung.	
Cigar ...	umhoin homlam	... ...	... ...	(*Gal.*) talomme.		
Cinnamon ...	tjá-ven.					
Circle ...	... ...	... ...	salōt.			
Citron ...	karo-eit ...	... ...	kamang ...	... ...	tjin.	
Claim ...	... ...	... ...	hahe.			
Clap (*hands*) ...	... ...	... ...	... ...	... ...	... ...	to-ko-kay.
Claw ...	kishoa.					
Clay ...	pi-et ...	... ...	piæt.			
Clean (81) ...	(81) i-tju-ik ...	... ...	tsieki ... akhik-tsie kité (*spiritually*).	... ...	... ...	rar-kay. tjatkay.
Cleanliness ...	... ...	... ...	tsie kité.			
Clever ...	léap ...	... ...	... ...	... ...	... ...	ar-ka-ber-rin-ga.
Climb ...	ut-tjat.					
Clock ...	tanak-rām ...	... ...	... ...	... ...	rap.	
Cloth (82) ...	lō-e; leinshe ... (82) (*strip of cl-*) lam œl.	... ...	longhaat ... (*blue cl-*) nâale.	... ...	holōn.	
Cloud ...	galahaie ...	... ...	tahihaal ...	... ...	gnó-e ...	tar'-gar-da.
	(*F. E. T.*) mifoian	... ...	... ...	... ...	... ...	(*O.H.B.*)boroda.
Close ...	... ...	... ...	... ...	... ...	... ...	(*O.H.B.*)lageea.
Clypeaster ...	jeng.					
Clove ...	shis-tjingi.					
Coal ...	som-joang kom-duṅg-ge.	... ...	tamâai ... tamia.	(*Gal.*) tamoaie.		

The vowels are sounded as in German or Hindustani; *j* as *y* in 'yard;' *ei* and *ai* are sounded like 'eye;' *au* as in 'Auge' (German); *æ* as *ai* in 'fair;' *œ* as in 'Oel' (German); *ch* soft as *ch* in 'loch.'

75.—*Novara, 'malao;' it means 'a string of beads.'*
76.—*Burmese.*
77.—*E. H. Man, 'hai yoo nang?'*
78.—*Galatea, Schowra, 'dja.'*
79.—*Fontana, 'aptejo.'*
80.—*deRff., Schowra, 'kapang.'*
81.—*Gal. 'efoa.'*
82.—*Fontana; strip of cloth 'lanoa.'*

English Words.	The Nancowry Dialect.	Great Nicobar.	Teressa by M. Plaisant.	Car Nicobar.	Inland Race 'Shobængs.'	Andaman Words.	Remarks.
Coast ...	kaje-tjuk ka-jija	... ...	tsio-matahæt.				
Coat (83) ...	(83) kaujut ...	... ...	... ...	... ...	tanhaï.		
Cock (84) ...	(84) kamóe kon.						
Cockroach ...	la-mashá.						
Cocoanut (85) (86) ...	(*ripe c-*) gnoat ...	... ...	... ...	... ...	(*ripe-c*) katel.		
	(*green c-*) jenong	... ...	jenong ...	... ...	(*green-c*) hóa.		
	(*kernel of c-*) hint-jeng.	... ...	(*de Rff., green c-*) kâhauk.				
	(*husk of c-*) kataw	... ...	... ...	... ...	(*husk of c.*) hint-jeng.		
	(*c-tree*) oglau ojuu	... ...	(*c-tree*) huveang	(*c-tree*) ta-āuk.			
	(*nuts*) jong-o-jau.						
	(85) (*ghee-c*) haján	... ...	(*empty-c*) nlong hâ.				
			(*prepare a c-*) nlong tê.				
Cold ...	patjau kaæ ...	... ...	... ...	... ...	ho-enjūp kaiñg	choe'-ke-kay.	
	hesh ...	... ...	... ...	... ...	tjahuk.		
Collect ...	... ...	... ...	hâahé.				
			kuket-ta-ieng-khiuk (*bring together in one spot*).				
Comb ...	kanoat.						
	kanewap.						
Come ...	ka-é-té-ró ...	... ...	(*arrive*) reugk ...	Gal. (*came*) tāē mattāē.	wén ...	keth-ne-gra-o-kay.	
	hængshe ...	... ...	(*approach*) hem	... ...	kutta	minnikatsh.	
						(*come away*) mo-cho-weet-kay.	
						(*c-and play*) mo'-cho-me-jurj-kay.	
Companion ...	... ...	... ...	hehang.				
			huleanga pâhê.				

Complete ...	omtôhm ...	... ...	tæt, theunghatæt	... ...	gœ-et.	
Concertina ...	danang.					
Condemn ...	... ...	... ...	nphé-ta-khiuk-hi-vi (*stop in place of the spirit*).			
Confined ...	... ...	... ...	(*be-c*) kahia ...	... ...	... ...	(*be-c*) (*O.H.B.*) ad-aleeka.
Consent ...	... ...	... ...	hehōt vetsen.			
Contract ...	... ...	... ...	hālā.			
Cook ...	... ...	... ...	... ...	... ...	... ...	jo-e-kay; (*O. H. B.*) ur-jooaka. (*O. H. B.* booj) (*c ing utensil*).
Cool ...	... ...	... ...	... ...	... ...	... ...	(*O.H.B.*)alara.
Coppermoney (*vide* Cash).	Sancta Maria ...	... ...	prata.			
Coral-lime ...	shun ...	... ...	... ...	... ...	kabev.	
Cork ...	kanjān ...	... ...	kafn'. kiak.			
Corner ...	(*E. H. M.*) ongkaung.					
Corpse ...	... ...	... ...	páhé kamapæt ...	... ...	... ...	uklike.
Cover ...	(*E. H. M.*) oke	... ...	huruh.			
Couch ...	... ...	... ...	... ...	... ...	... ...	dootram (*O. X. N.*)
Cough ...	tjahoā ...	... ...	kinfat ...	... ...	o-ong ...	udagda.
	hagl ...	... ...	... ...	... ...	... ...	o'thor-kay.
Count ...	harrow ...	... ...	haraâk ...	(*Gal.*) aiel ...	panne.	
Cousin ...	... ...	... ...	eonang.			
Coward ...	(*E. H. M.*) pum-maboin.					
Crab ...	kinong; (*F.E.T.*) kālan-gei.					

The vowels are sounded as in German or Hindustani; *j* as *y* in 'yard;' *ei* and *ai* are sounded like 'eye;' *au* as in 'Auge' (German); *æ* as *ai* in 'fair;' *œ* as in 'Oel' (German); *ch* soft as *ch* in 'loch.'"

83.—*Fontana. 'Chanlo,' obsolete!*

84.—*Novara. 'Kamooe-koep?' The stay of the 'Novara' at Nancowry was very short!*

85.—*Ghee means 'Indian melted butter.' The nuts I call 'ghee cocoanuts' are peculiar to the Nicobars, and are considered a great rarity. They do not grow hard and taste nearly as horrible as ghee. The tree that bears them will sometimes produce good nuts with hard kernels. They are used at feasts for offerings.*

86.—*deRff. Schowra green cocoanut 'kâhauk.'*

English Words.	The Nancowry Dialect.	Great Nicobar.	Teressa by M. Plaisant.	Car Nicobar.	Inland race 'Shobængs.'	Andaman Words.	Remarks.
Cradle ...	... ...	... ...	khiuk khinion (*place for child*). nghoik.				
Crayfish ...	mulhœl ...	... ...	... ...	... ...	mokœ.		
Create ...	... ...	... ...	huhé, huhomi.				
Creek ...	... ...	... ...	... ...	... ...	... ...	(*O.H. B.*) jeeg.	
Crooked ...	kedāl ...	... ...	kirhol ...	... ...	wel ta œ.		
Cross ...	hatein pejā.						
Crossbrow ...	foing ...	... ...	... ...	... ...	fenji.		
Crow ...	... ...	... ...	... ...	... ...	... ...	bart'-car-da.	
Crush ...	... ...	... ...	nkhâa, khâa. pataxi, rakn.				
Cry ...	tjīm ...	... ...	hæ hægne. tikâat kahehole...	... ...	... ...	tiek'-e-kay. te-gi-ké. takeeka (*O. H. B.*)	
Cultivate ...	wējom						
Cup ...	piteng ...	... ...	... ...	... ...	... ...	o-da-da (*nautilus-shell*).	
Cupidity ...	... ...	... ...	hehomang-ta-ra-mc-khia (*desire after every tree*).				
Custom ...	(*E.H.M.*) tatoichu	... ...	mhæne. khianti, (*s*) khi-ansi.				
Cut ...	ontoang, olkal ...	... ...	fhâa, nfâ, nká ...	... ...	kadenji ...	col-kay kapike ig-nar-le-kay (*O.H.B.*) chool-kă.	
Cyclone ...	(*F.E.T.*) Oo-tala. (*E.H.M.*) hoora-sheh.						
D.							
Dagger ...	sanéat ...	... ...	samiñ (*e*) ...	... ...	ki.		
Dah (*Burmese knife*).	kidume ... kidjumeh.	... ...	... ...	... ...	kidum-nafœ.		

Dance ...	katoka ...	... ...	... ...	... ...	... ...	ko-e-kay tirrepu. (*O. H. B.*) ra-meeda.
Danger ...	tjue ja jan ...	... ...	rhamang (*fear*).			
Dare ...	... ...	... ...	hat-rhamang.			
Dark ...	tjōkūl ...	... ...	titial ...	... ...	... ...	goo-'roog-da.
Darkness ...	Nov. doochool. (*F.E.T.*) toochool.					
Daub ...	o-ak.					
Daughter ...	koñ enkana ...	... ...	nkênhje-kuan.			
Daughter-in-law..	nkan koñ ...	... ...	nkênhje-kuan.			
Day (87) ...	(87) hæng (*i. e., sun-light*).	... ...	hungi ...	... ...	he-it; ta-a ...	el-la-war-kay.
	tot, (*counting days*).	... ...	... ...	... ...	... ...	aladea(*O.H.B.*)
	sejú lang (*the day after tomorrow*).	... ...	schæht (*day after tomorrow*).	... ...	shenekaîn (*day after tomorrow*)	(*O.H.B.*) choekă (*daybreak*).
	linhæng (*today*).					
	manjúe (*yester-day*).					
	tensagi (*daylight*) (*Fontana*).					
Dead ...	kapá ...	... ...	kapæt ...	... ...	ba-ó.	e-poo'-koo-yar-bar-da.
Deaf ...	tjit jang ...	... ...	... ...	... ...	... ...	
Debase ...	... ...	... ...	wit fhôt.			
Deceitful ...	kaló ...	... ...	... ...	... ...	bala-íít.	
Decree ...	tjarjo ...	... ...	ivihoatse.			
Deep ...	Novara, thjajas (*E. H. M.*) oal.	... ...	khiâa.			
Defend ...	... ...	... ...	habâai-			
Deity ...	de-us iwi. ...	... ...	... ...	... ...	tasheng.	
Delicate ...	... ...	... ...	hat-nhin.			

The vowels are sounded as in German or Hindustani; *j* as *y* in 'yard;' *ei* and *ai* are sounded like 'eye;' *au* as in 'Auge' (German); *æ* as *ai* in 'fair;' *œ* as in 'Oel' (German); *ch* soft as *ch* in 'loch.'

87.—'*hæn*' *day* (*Rosen*, 1834).

English Words.	The Nancowry Dialect.	Great Nicobar.	Teressa by M. Plaisant.	Car Nicobar.	Inland race 'Shobængs.'	Andaman Words.	Remarks.
Delicious ...	shéang ...	... ...	... ...	... ...	sheit.		
Demand ...	oljōle ..	... ...	hahē-ten.				
Demi-egret ...	(F.E.T.) khū-ark.						
Demon (88)	(88) iwi ...	... ...	hivi ...	... ...	pawi.		
Denmark (89) ...	(89) Tanemāru.						
Deny ...	... ...	... ...	hat-ghēn vetsen.				
Descend ...	onhang ...	... ...	hotsiét ...	(Gal.) iaange.			
Devil (90) ...	(90) (Hænsel.) eewee.	... ...	... ...	... ...	tasheng ...	errum-chow-galla.	
Dew ...	dju-shuwang.						
Dhoty (91) ...	(E. H. M.) loih-sharong.						
Die ...	kapá ...	... ...	kapæt ...	... ...	... ...	oc-ko-lee-kay. (O.H.B.)ookoo-leekă.	
Difference ...	karōke ...	... ...	nreng' ntsie.				
Difficult	(E. H. M.) gnia-nayun.	... ...	hunhaug-heng.				
Dig ...	... ...	... ...	... ...	... ...	... ...	(O.H.B.) koop.	
Diminish ...	... ...	... ...	hehetsi.				
Dirt ...	œlgh omat ...	... ...	hehū.				
Dirty ...	(F. E. T.) eu ...	... ...	hifū-heu.				
Disapprove ...	... ...	... ...	hat-hehōt. hatalang.				
Discover ...	... ...	... ...	op.				
Disease ...	pomkeie ...	... ...	... ...	... ...	o-eñg-ha poak. ...	ek-bung-gikay.	
Disgust ...	... ...	... ...	hoh'hangatsike.				
Dishonest ...	kaló	... ...	hat-tulan-atse ...	olĉi ...	kashitje.		
Disobedient ...	... ...	... ...	(be d-) miki-haïe.				
Displease ...	... ...	... ...	hoh'hangatsike.				
Distant ...	hœ-e ...	... ...	... ...	... ...	... ...	(O. H. B.) il-lurpa.	
Distribute ...	... ...	... ...	aluha ...	... ...	... ...	(O.H.B.) wālkă.	

Dive ...	hamp.						
Divide ...	harrow ...	... ...	tolæt (*hew to pieces*).				
Do ...	tjit akah (*do not know*)	... ...	aluha. kit akah (*do not know*).	tji tjalañ ...	... ...	ó-kay-yar-ba(*do not touch it*). on-kar-nar-kay (*do not do that*). ar-ka-wel-lup-kay (*I have done enough*).	
Doctor ...	manló-ine ...	... ...	... ...	... ...	penlunne.		
Dog (92) (93) ...	(92) âhm ...	... ...	hōm ...	(*Hamilton*) támam (*Gal.*) amm.	kūp ...	be'-bee* ...	* "Be'-bee"—dog. It is often said at the Andamans that this word has been adopted by a mistake from the Hindustani; it means 'a woman' in this language. This seems to me very unlikely, just as unlikely as the old story that the Andaman 'negrito' should come from African slaves wrecked on these coasts in a Portuguese vessel. Their 'kjök kenmöddings' prove that they have been longer in these islands than the Portuguese have been in India.
Dollar ...	para.						
Door ...	kakani. foang.						
Double ...	... ...	... ...	iang-amōk. hehemōnk. kahâak.				
Dove ...	*vide* Pigeon ...	... ...					
Down (94) ...	pūje (*sit d-*) ...	... ...	... ...	(*Gal.*) hoinræ (*sit d-*)	gñidé (*sit d-*)... kantœv (*i. e., wait*).	lot'-te-kay. theg'-ge-kay (*put d-*) o-cho-thoow (*move d-*) arth-bul. akadóekay (*sit d-*). arth-bul-ler-ge kay (*lie d-*).	

The vowels are sounded as in German or Hindustani; *j* as *y* in 'yard;' *ei* and *ai* are sounded like 'eye;' *au* as in 'Auge' (German); *æ* as *ai* in 'fair;' *œ* as in 'Oel' (German); *ch* soft as *ch* in 'loch'.

88.—*In the meaning of the Greek δαίμων.*

89.—*They have a very distinct recollection of the Danes.*

90.—*I do not believe that the spirits which the Nicobarese fear could be called devils. They are the 'manes.' That however the Moravian missionary might take that view is easy to understand, and others as the Revd. Barbe, Novara, and E. H. Man did not speak the language at the time when they made their collections.*

91.—*Is a cloth which a Hindoo wears in lieu of trowsers.*

92.—*So also Rosen.*

93.—*Wallace, Mysol, 'yem.'*

94.—*deRff., Schowra, 'poshe.' Gal, Little Nicobar, 'kantai.'* } *sit down.*

English Words.	The Nancowry Dialect.	Great Nicobar.	Teressa by M. Plaisant.	Car Nicobar.	Inland race 'Shobængs.'	Andaman Words.	Remarks.
Draw ...	... ...	... ...	táak ...	... ...	... ...	do-e'-kay.	
Dream ...	en-fó-a ...	... ...	nfâa-huho ...	omfæ ...	konfoang tœ.		
Dress ...	... ...	... ...	kinlôh.				
Drink (95) ...	top, pem ...	... ...	nhiong ...	(95) ka-œt ...	laha-e ...	wil'-lit-kay.	
	top umhoin (*smoke tobacco*).	... ...	... ...	... ...	koak ...	willike; tjatkay (*O.H.B.*)oligka.	
Drive ...	harjan (*d-away*)..	... ...	khui (*dr. away*).				
Drunk ...	hujōé ...	... ...	huhehohé ...	mashōta ...	kalœ.		
Duck ...	wét ...	... ...	bâté.				
Dumb ...	... ...	... ...	hat nheōle ...	... ...	... ...	or-ko-mool-we-kay.	
Dust ...	piét ...	... ...	hæhia (*chihiá*).				
E.							
Ear (96) (97) ...	(96) nang ... (97) ijé, itjei (*earsticks*).	... ...	nang ... kot, kogn, mifæ sanamnang (*ear-spoon*).	... ...	gũa ... tjũe (*ear-ache*) ijei (*ear-sticks*)	e-poo'-koo-da. (*O.H.B.*) pokoo.	
Early ...	al haki.						
Earring (98) ...	(98) (*E. H. M.*) eetchai.						
Earth (99) ...	(99) oal mattei ...	... ...	matah æt (*world*) lenku (*e-quake*).	... ...	hong ...	(*O. H. B.*) gārā. (*O. H.* ...) boo-gooka (*bury in the earth*).	
East (100) ...	(100) fol ... haé fol (*north-east monsoon*).	... ...	... ...	... ...	komdœng(*north-east monsoon*).		
Ease oneself ...	... ...	... ...	... ...	... ...	... ...		
Easy ...	(*E. H. M.*) too yu-yun.	... ...	râatk ivi.	... ...	... ...	(*O. H. B.*) ric-hiaka.	

Eat (101) (102) (103).	(101) auk nôk ...	kanjap ...	(102) ungha ...	(*Hamilton*) gnia	nak ...	(103) mækré, maekay tick-boot-ray (*satisfied with eating*). el-la-air-kay. (*O. H. B.*) aka-waitka.
Ebb-tide ...	(*Novara*) tchoh...	... ...	... ...	... ...	... ...	
Ebony ...	komtjing.					
Edible ...	h i k a é (*e-bird's nests*).					
Eel ...	lōan ...	... ...	paivâat ...	... ...	enkét.	
Egg ...	hoja ...	... ...	bæó ...	(*Gal.*) laal ...	... ...	mo'-lo-da.
Eight ...	nfóan ...	... ...	nfoon ...	(*Gal.*) hævret ...	atti.	
Eighteen ...	shom-nfōan.					
Eighty ...	fuan umdjomé.					
Either—or ...	hat-khiuk-khiuka					
Elbow ...	det un kéang ...	... ...	reankiang. sekong.			
Elder ...	... ...	... ...	hyhabo.			
Elephant ...	lé fante.					
Elephantiasis ...	wotoang ...	... ...	... ...	... ...	bashoï.	
Eleven ...	shom héang ...	... ...	iaeang. iang-tôn.			
Else ...	... ...	... ...	nreng'n tsie. hâat etâ (*elsewhere*).			
Embers ...	omak.					
Employ ...	... ...	... ...	vi, vi huk.			
Empty ...	gnuñg ...	... ...	... ...	... ...	hœi.	

The vowels are sounded as in German or Hindustani; *j* as *y* in 'yard;' *ei* and *ai* are sounded like 'eye;' *au* as in 'Auge' (German); *æ* as *ai* in 'fair;' *œ* as in 'Oel' (German); *ch* soft as *ch* in 'loch.'

95.—*Hamilton, Car Nicobar, 'okk.' Gal., drinking vessel, 'dhjugar.'*
96.—*Wallace, 'Mysol,' tenaan.*
97.—*So also Rosen.*
98.—*Does not mean 'ear-rings,' but the sticks they wear in their big-bored ears.*
99.—*Rosen, 'voal-mat tai.' E. H. M., 'doo?'; doubtful.*
100.—*Rosen, 'full.'*
101.—*Fontana, 'hanino.'*
102.—*Teressa, deRff. 'nja kahœ' (I eat).*
103.—*Little Andaman, deRff., 'makui lélé' (I am satisfied).*

English Words.	The Nancowry Dialect.	Great Nicobar.	Teressa by M. Plaisant.	Car Nicobar.	Inland race "Shobængs."	Andaman Words.	Remarks.
Encampment (104)	... ...	... ...	... ...	... ...	... ...	(104) (*O. H. B.*) aēr.	
Enceinte ...	... ...	... ...	... ...	... ...	... ...	(*O. H. B.*) ar-bodida.	
End ...	... ...	... ...	lét, gon-(*to e-*) mang (*the e-*)				
English ...	In-glæsi.						
Enough (105) ...	léat ...	... ...	tet hâat ...	... ...	gna ho-e ...	(105) thoo-roo-mar-ba.	
Enter ...	... ...	... ...	vetsen. hiāñ sang'n. iatet.				
Equal ...	oign.						
Escape ...	... ...	... ...	rhâne, rhæne.				
Esteem ...	... ...	... ...	hehohang.				
Evening ...	engse shup heng (*just before sunset*).	... ...	atam ...	... ...	gñalāk he-i ...	(*O. H. B.*) alā-rect.	
	ladi'-eje-(*sunset*) ...	... ...	ladije.				
	hatam (*while it is dark*).						
Everyone ...	omtôhm ...	... ...	râme pâhé ... ta-râme.	... ...	gœ-et.		
Everywhere ...	... ...	... ...	râme-khiuk. ta-râme-khiuk.				
Evil ...	hat lapôh ...	... ...	net lopāh. khiak ghen net lo-pāh kā vi pâ-hé (*speak evil of a person*).	... ...	gna kœ ...	er-ram-chow-galla (*the evil spirit*).	
European ...	kalén (*foreigner*).						
Exceed ...	... ...	... ...	tan hihaai.				
Exchange ...	umkom si tjænmé	... ...	metam ; sehia.				
Expensive ...	... ...	... ...	lhâak.				
Experience ...	... ...	... ...	kom-te-akah.				

Expert ...	... ...	... ...	liap-tān-râme (*towards every one*). l'hōlevi (*be-e-*).			
Eye (106) ...	(106) olmat ... (*F. E. T.*) all-mā-nīka.	... ...	emat ... iniang-te-emat... (*one-eyed*).	G. olmat ... (*pluralis*) oalmang	hinmat	e-darl'-da. dal-da.
Eyebrows ...	aukmat ... pujôl olmat.	... ...	... ...	(*Gal.*) drugmat .	behol hinmat.	
Eyelash ...	kat feit ...	... ...	huk-emat.			
Eyelid ...	hinop olmat ...	... ...	... ...	oñg ade.		
F.						
Face (107) ...	(107) tjokahæ ...	... ...	mēt ...	(*Gal.*) khua ...	gño tjue.	
Fair ...	ta-it.					
Fall ...	pom-fuk-se ... pom-takse ... talœhe ...	... ...	khavæ ; khâa ... (nkâa). tsigamāng (*fall on the knees*).	... ...	tashe ... köm-tā.	(*O. H. B.*) apar-ka.
Falsehood ...	mi-tā-i ...	... ...	mitaö ...	... ...	... ...	ar-kun-yon-ger-te-kay. idjaj kay.
Fan ...	hanei-ahé; (*F. E. T.*) iffooee. hania.	... ...	... ...	... ...	kan-fi.	
Far ...	hœ-i ; how-i ...	... ...	hâaik. ...	... ...	gña-e-kō ...	ar-par'-lar-da. (*O. H. B.*) illur-pa (*f-away*). (*O H. B.*) la-gēēa (*not f-*).
Farewell (108) (109) (110)	(108) tawatse de mederœ. (109) be-ha ré. (110) jetju-tawatse.	... ...	... ...	... ...	tjue.	

The vowels are sounded as in German or Hindustani ; *j* as *y* in 'yard ;' *ei* and *ai* are sounded like 'eye'; *au* as in 'Auge' (German); *æ* as *ai* in 'fair'; *œ* as in 'Oel' (German); *ch* soft as *ch* in 'loch.'

104.—*Means also 'place of rest,'* (*O. H. B.*)
105.—*Little Andaman, 'mæmavel,' enough,* (*deRff.*)
106.—*Malay, 'mata.'*
107.—*Rosen, 'djakah'* (*so also F. E. T.*)
108. -*The guest.*
109.—*The host.*
110.—*Fontana, 'kala-kala-younde?'*

English Words.	The Nancowry dialect.	Great Nicobar.	Teressa by M. Plaisant.	Car Nicobar.	Inland race Shobaengs.	Andaman Words.	Remarks.
Fast ...	lo-á (*quick*) ...	... ...	... ...	... ...	aha aha ...	*O. H. B.* mameeka (*fast asleep*). *O.H.B.* roneka (*faster*).	
Fat ...	onhéang (*lard*)	... ...	hul'hu (*lard*) ...	... ...	pashō-eī ...	arb-par-tar-tho ga'.	
	pontjerah ...	... ...	nehang ...	... ...	... ...	*O. H. B.* pata.	
	to-foa-po ...	... ...	tahang.				
Father ...	tjia ...	... ...	iæt; kaiet (*old man*).	... ...	dōla ...	mi-o-la.	
			pap ...	... ...	... ...	ar-o-de-ræ.	
Father-in-law ...	*Gal.* komiahtje...	... ...	kumhje.				
Favour ...	... ...	... ...	tahnihætsen.				
Fear ...	pohoa ...	... ...	rhamang ... he-kapèt (*fear of death*).	... ...	pa-œ-a.		
Feast ...	milœ ...	... ...	hatnâak; hellamong long.	... ...	enméañg.		
Feather (111) ...	(111) pujôl.						
Female ...	enkāna ...	... ...	... ...	... ...	ojū, penhūt ...	*O.H.B.* apaila Do. abara (*unmarried*). Do. abchabil (*married*). djerri djobda (*maiden*).	
Fence ...	katang ...	... ...	... ...	... ...	... ...	poó-too-da.	
Fern ...	dela-tō-in ...	... ...	... ...	... ...	haná.		
Fever ...	tōo ...	... ...	... ...	... ...			
Few (111A) ...	ti tjoha, *F. E. T.* hat-orro-assi (111A). samet dat shéen.	... ...	kna, ki, kôa.	... ...	tein; fōp ...	arb-ou'-yar-da abæt.	
Field ...	lenki ...	... ...	fô.				

Fifteen ...	shom tanein.					
Fifty ...	am-umdjomé ruktei.	... ...	tani-tón.			
Fight (112)(113)	pomōn ...	... ...	pamoiñ (*a f-*) ...	... ...	hoheengbo ...	tikræl.
	(112) kajué (*fighting stick*).	... ...	pamoiñ (*to f-*) ...	... ...	he-enjit.	
	(113) kamili (*fighting cap*).					
File ...	tané jan.					
Fill ...	harfut.					
Find ...	komb ...	... ...	kum.			
Fine ...	... ...	... ...	lopah hat-nhin.			
Finger (113 A)	ganetei (*finger*)	... ...	... ...	*Gal.* kunte ...	... ...	*O.H.B.* koroda.
	mandú-e (*thumb*)					
	manshonka (*2nd finger*).					
	monju og gñi (*long finger*).					
	tanoëmandæntje (*4th finger*).					
	mandæntje (*little finger*).	... ...	maniæije (*little finger*).			
Finish (114) ...	léat, go-ong ...	... ...	... ...	... ...	hoi ...	(114) *O. H. B.* urleecutka.
Finn ...	ho-a-la-tæ. kashu ... han-tahá.	... ...	... ...	... ...	ok.	
Fire ...	he-ó-c ...	... ...	akapset (*light a fire*).	*Ham.* t'amia ...	... ...	*O.H.B.* surun (*a light*).
	omāk (*embers*)' ...	... ...	karhû tamoī (*strong fire*). pala.	... ...	... ...	*O. H. B.* edal (*a f-*).

The vowels are sounded as in German or Hindustani; *j* as *y* in 'yard;' *ei* and *ai* are sounded like 'eye;' *au* as in 'Auge' (German); *æ* as *ai* in 'fair;' *œ* as in 'Oel' (German); *ch* soft as *ch* in 'loch.'

111.—*Novara, 'anet-layeebery' means a pen. One of the mistakes liable to occur, when a vocabulary is to be made of a new language in a week!*

111*A*.—*Vide* Much *and* Many. *This word of Mr. Tuson's is only the negative added to 'many'!*

112.—*Long stick, steeped in pig's blood and rolled in sand. This is used in all petty feuds.*

113.—*A well-padded hat worn in their fights to prevent any heads being broken.*

113*A*.—*Schowra., deRff., 'ko-en-no-i.'*

114.—*Little Andaman' deRff., 'makui lélé.'*

English Words.	The Nancowry Dialect.	Great Nicobar.	Teressa by M. Plaisant.	Car Nicobar.	Inland race 'Shobængs.'	Andaman Words.	Remarks.
Fireplace (115) ...	(115) gñi heóe (*house for f-*).	... ...	... ...	(*Gal.*) sittam.			
Firewood ...	he-ā-ka ...	... ...	hok inæ ...	(*Gal.*) kuanghere	... ...	chár-pa-da; bini.	
Fish (116) ...	(116) kā ...	... ...	huhot; khâ ...	(*Ham.*) ka ...	gna ...	yartha'da.	
	oktoakā (*to f-with line*).	... ...	karah ...	... ...	... ...	ukra	
						kapokay.	
Fish-hook ...	karau hat lot ...	... ...	karah.				
Fish-spear ...	hokpāk (*wooden f.*)	... ...	... ...	... ...	kade kohaign.		
	miá (*forked iron f.*)	... ...	... ...	... ...	gagan.		
	monheangte shanein (*one barbed iron f.*)						
Fist ...	... ...	... ...	kuhihu.				
Fit ...	idi.						
Five ...	tanei ...	... ...	tani ...	(*Gal.*) tanein ...	deñg.		
	tanein.						
Flag ...	fehnwæ.						
	henwæ.						
Flame ...	tjul.						
Flannel ...	kañg-i.						
Flat ...	œngshe.						
Flatten ...	... ...	... ...	rhâam.				
Flea ...	shēi.						
Flesh ...	ahan ...	... ...	lupā ...	(*Gal.*) ghantéra	ke-inje.		
Flight ...	taæ.						
Flint ...	hindæl.						
Flog ...	ori.						
Flood ...	hev ...	... ...	... ...	... ...	gœt-lup ...	ella-boo-'kay.	
Flower ...	shi ...	... ...	eang schiâ (*flower bough*).				
	kanla na ōng ...	... ...	hi; eang-khiâ.				
Flute ...	(*Gal.*) henhæl ...	... ...	neheurle.				
Fly (*a fly*) (117 A)	Júe (117 A) ...	... ...	... ...	... ...	... ...	(*O.H.B.*) bomee.	
Fly (*to fly*) ...	(*F.E.T.*) haingna	... ...	ta æ ...	... ...	... ...	war-'ter-pe-kay?	
Flying-fish ...	monkeang.						

Foliage ...	... ...	... ...	huhato.			
Follow ...	... ...	... ...	tsang.			
Food ...	auk nôk ...	... ...	hat nâak ...	... ...	kakéā ...	mæk.
			mahehâat.			
Foot (117) ...	(117) la ...	... ...	K (*s*) aminâat (1,000 *foot*).	gundron ...	tjœk ...	on-parg'-da.
	ol-la (*foot-sole*)...	... ...	... ...	... ...	... ...	paguda.
	hinkāp-la (*foot-rings*).					
Forbid ...	ole ta la ...	... ...	hahâai ...	enkoi ...	en kō-i ...	ig-moo-'goo-da-.
Forehead (118) ...	(118) lal.					
Foreigner ...	kaleñg ; kalein ...	... ...	... ...	pohœn.	... ...	(*O.H.B.*)talama.
Forest ...	oltjoā ...	... ...	khiâ ...	... ...	ong-a-do ...	(*O.H.B.*)ajeekă.
Forget ...	pæñg-gña-to ...	... ...	fuongato ; l'hag'n	... ...	pūel.	
			pengatt ...	... ...		
Forgive ...	shom-la-ta.					
Fork ...	tjanæp.					
Formerly ...	tirām ...	... ...	huhag'n.			
Fortify ...	... ...	... ...	nlēn.			
Forty ...	a inein (2 *times* 20)	... ...	fue-tôn ...	... ...	a deñp.	
	ām umdjomé (2 *times* 20 *twenties*).					
Four ...	fuán ...	... ...	foue, fen, fuan ...	... ...	fōn.	
	a tafúel (2 *pairs*)	... ...	foan.			
Fourteen ...	shōm-fuan ...	... ...	iang-tôn-foue.			
	ishāt-tafuel (7 *pairs*).					
Fowl (119) (120)...	(120) kamó-e ...	... ...	... ...	(119) (*Ham.*) hay-am.		
Fox ...	mognéaka (*flying f*).	... ...	... ...	... ...	kanwam.	
Frame ...	... ...	... ...	mang.			

The vowels are sounded as in German or Hindustani; *j* as *y* in 'yard;' *ei* and *ai* are sounded like 'eye;' *au* as in 'Auge' (German); *æ* as *ai* in 'fair;' *œ* as in 'Oel' (German); *ch* soft as *ch* in 'loch.'

115.—*Gal.* '*Umag.*
116.—*Rosen.* '*Ghâ.*'
117.—*Rosen.* '*Lâh.*
117A.—*Big fly*, '*huncoat,*' (*F. E. T.*)
118.—*Rosen.* '*Lâl.*'
119.—*Malay.*
120.—*Rosen.* '*Tafo'ák.*'

English Words.	The Nancowry dialect.	Great Nicobar.	Teressa by M. Plaisant.	Car Nicobar.	Inland race 'Shorængs.'	Andaman words.	Remarks.
Fresh ...	dhéagh fau (*f-water*).	... ...	fââb-dag (*fresh water*).	... ...	dui (*fresh water*).		
Friend ...	(*E. H. M.*) kaiyol	... ...	kahihot-komivi mivi.	... ...	... ...	padoo.	
Frighten ...	... ...	... ...	pahāt.				
Frog ...	hakang ...	... ...	... ...	... ...	o-wō-a ...	(*O. H. B.*) rupun.	
From ...	abhi (*from hence*).						
Fruit ...	jong ...	... ...	... ...	... ...	... ...	an'-ga-rar-da.	
Full ...	pōsh ; po ; pahaé ānh-hoál.	... ...	... ...	... ...	tein-le ..	(*O. H. B.*) tirboot ká (*satisfied.*)	
Full-moon ...	ful ...	... ...	renāāng.				
Future ...	seju ...	... ...	tsihé.				
G.							
Gait ...	... ...	... ...	kalamā.				
Gape ...	hinâp tigñāp. ...	... ...	fââb ...	... ...	anāp.		
Garden ...	jōm ...	... ...	hæm.				
Gather ...	... ...	... ...	hâahé				
Geccoo ...	kolokiakke hōjé. ...	... ...	... ...	... ...	gœ-it.		
Get up ...	kœv-me ...	... ...	... ...	*Gal.* kiaalĕrĕ ...	tau-inn ...	bo-e-kay. (*O. H. B.*) kapeeka.	
Gift ...	... ...	... ...	tahnihætsen.				
Gild ...	... ...	... ...	homlaame.				
Gill ...	taboan.						
Ginger ...	enhang.						
Gird ...	... ...	nlen					
Girl ...	holeajing ...	... ...	... ...	... ...	... ...	appaila (*woman*). djerri-djōbda (*maiden*).	
	kanjom enkāna.						

Give ...	kjuan hatta ...	... ...	kētē; kæt ... nrongkté; sâht (g-back).	... ... /	... ... /	ai-nar'-kay. (O. H. B.) omokă	
Glad ...	... ...	... ...	... ...	... ...	... ...	or-tho-yil-lar-kay edjaj.	
Glass ...	labetwā (big) ... wétéré (small).	sume (Wicks) ...	... ...	... ...	njanteré.		
Gnat ...	mihōje ...	... ...	... ...	... ...	bishūeñg.		
Go (121) ...	(121) tju ... ju tju (I go or a good boy).	... ... /	ave; heâgn; thin hafot sag'n (go on board).	Gal. kerahiere ... /	... ...	onkay. (O. H. B.) itaree (go out, i. e., a light).	
			iatet (go in) ...	... ...	... ...	dar-rine-leck-now-lar-kay (go up a tree).	
			thiudi-okei ...	... ...	... ...	mo-'cho-on-kay (let us go).	
Goat ...	kaperæ.						
Goblet ...	tajak.						
God ...	Hœnsel knallen iwi; teos.	... ...	... ...	... ...	bawi ...	thot-ma.	
Gold ...	golmōre ... enlùne.	... ...	homlaame.				
Good ...	lapōé ...	... ...	helang; l'hâak,	... ...	shai-tong; kœ	beringada.*	*These three forms are all correct and are understood by the natives that visit the Settlements. I have on purpose given three different spellings to show how gradually words steal into the Andamanese dialects.
	shéang (ie., sweet)	... ...	lopah ... tsiang (sweet): tulan.	... ... /	... ... /	bæringada. (O. H. B.) baree gudda.	
Good-bye (122) (123).	(122) ju tju; ta-watse de me de rœ. (123) bé haré.						

The vowels are sounded as in German or Hindustani; *j* as *y* in 'yard;' *ei* and *ai* are sounded like 'eye;' *au* as in 'Auge' (German); *æ* as *ai* in 'fair;' *œ* as in 'Oel' (German); *ch* soft as *ch* in 'loch.'

121.—*A. C. Man. 'Eetakke,' means 'to sleep.' Mr. Man was only there about three weeks. He collected 86 words, of which 23 were new ones.*

122.—*The departing guest.*
123.—*The host.*

English Words.	The Nancowry Dialect.	Great Nicobar.	Teressa by M. Plaisant.	Car Nicobar.	Inland Race 'Shobængs.'	Andaman Words.	Remarks.
Goose ...	o-ko'-ang-ka.						The convict warders and others who have to communicate with these savages use a curious mixture of English-Hindustani interspersed with words of real Andaman origin. This they would like to pass off for the Andaman language, but many of the words as 'baree-gudda' for 'very good,' 'unchada' of the Hindustani 'uncha,' distinctly show that the Andamanese are just as good linguists as those with whom they have to transact business. 'Jarroowallahs' become 'Jarudawad das' or 'Jurra wuddahs.' These names are used of the mythical inland tribe that is believed to live close to the Port Blair Settlement. Lately the people of Little Andaman have been included under the same names.
Granddaughter ...	kōin koān ...	... ...	... ...	... ...	... ...	ardoati.	
Grandfather ...	tjōm kōnje ...	... ...	hadija.				
Grandmother ...	tjōm nkāna ...	... ...	habnhaât.				
Grandson ...	kōin koān ...	... ...	ahúhot ...	... ...	... ...	ardoati.	
Grass (124) ...	(124) shæn.						
Gratitude ...	haheha æng.						
Grave ...	ol ōle ...	... ...	... ...	... ...	hébāaje.		
Grease ...	onheam ...	... ...	... ...	... ...	ohōw.		
Great ...	orohatse (*in quantity*). kadū (*in size*).	... ...	... ...	... ...	bashœit ...	(*O. H. B.*) chanukda.	
Green ...	tjumóa ...	... ...	nâale ...	... ...	gœt.		
Grief ...	(*E. H. M.*) tjet; kei-tje-jen.	... ...	... ...	... ...	la-e-æt.		
Groan ...	(*E. H. M.*) ñjo-an	... ...	... ...	... ...	ka-it.		
Ground ...	tanæn ...	... ...	... ...	... ...	... ...	gar-'rar-da.	
Grow ...	... ...	... ...	hēhǎnē. rhônk.				
Guano ...	(*E. H. M.*) aing-ala-ah.						
Guard ...	... ...	... ...	hanhoume.				
Guava ...	gojāwa.						
Gum ...	*Rosen* baga-u.						
Gun ...	hindæl ... hinkok (*ship's gun*).	... ...	... ...	... ...	fung (*originally a bow*).		
Gunja (*Cannabis sativa.*)	kanīn ...	... ...	... ...	... ...	kafū.		
Gunpowder ...	taru.						
H.							
Hag (125) ...	(125) *Rosen* angana umjáha.						

Hair (126) ...	hankōjé; juôk; (*F. E. T.*) york.	... ...	hehok ...	(*Gal.*) kheui ...	hō ..	oth-pij-da.
	kajôl; pujol ...	... ...	... ...	... ...	... ...	tjōlda?
	hitōa (*hair-dress*)	... ...	... ...	... ...	... ...	(*O. H. B.*) peej-ga.
	wona kōēde (*h-whip of China-men*).	... ...	... ...	... ...	... ...	(*O. H. B.*) too-lea (*white h.*)
Half ...	oign ...	... ...	lā. mâhâa.			
Hammer ...	dom ...	... ...	renâam.			
Hand (127) (128)	(128) ganitei ...	... ...	lotoh iaale (*right h-*).	... ...	... ...	arng-co-ro-da koruda.
			munté; mukté ...	... ...	... ...	tóko-kay (*clap hands*).
Handkerchief ...	tanot hoang ...	... ...	... ...	... ...	tat onang ho.	
Handsome ...	(*E. H. M.*) ya maishehka.					
Hang ...	poka-on-lon'-ge...	... ...	hawnhōlĕt ...	... ...	kēt.	
Happy ...	(*E. H. M.*) yah-natau.	... ...	hāhé.			
Harbour ...	... ...	... ...	khiuk-khiniong (*i. e., ship's place*).			
Hard ...	... ...	... ...	kalet ...	... ...	... ...	wool-lun-tho-ga-da (*it blows hard*).
Hat ...	shapéau (*Malay*)	... ...	kerebusse.			
Hatch ...	... ...	... ...	buruh.			
Hatchet ...	enlóin ...	... ...	... ...	... ...	kandon njom.	
Hate ...	(*E. H. M.*) ha natau.	... ...	hoh'hangatsike...	... ...	... ...	or-ko-jan-ge-yar-bi-kay.
Have ...	ôt (*i. e., is*) ...	... ...	khjiang ...	(*Gal.*) nkiēne.		

The vowels are sounded as in German or Hindustani; *j* as *y* in 'yard;' *ei* and *ai* are sounded like 'eye;' *au* as in 'Auge' (German); *æ* as *ai* in 'fair;' *œ* as in 'Oel' (German); *ch* soft as *ch* in 'loch.'

124.—*E. H. Man.* '*Shen*' (*ordinary gr-*) '*opyooap*' (*jungle gr-*) '*shen-fo*' (*lalang gr-*)

125.—*Means* '*old woman.*'

126.—*Schowra, de Rff.*, '*héak;*' '*hin mein.*'

127.—*Schowra, de Rff.*, '*kot-nanōi.*'

128.—*Rosen.* '*Genās.*'

English Words.	The Nancowry dialect.	Great Nicobar.	Teressa by M. Plaisant.	Car Nicobar.	Inland race 'Shobængs.'	Andaman words.	Remarks.
Hawk ...	kalang-ok-joa ...	... ...	mifaie.				
He ...	anné ... an paju.	... ...	ané.				
Head (128 A) ...	gōi; kōi ...	... ...	gœh, kœh ... khui ...	... ...	po	otk-chai'-ter-da tshætada. (*O.H.B.*) cheta.	
Headache ...	tjok koi ...	... ...	khiak djak khūi	... ...	... ...	(*O. H. B.*) ik-bhoongeekā.	
Heap ...	... ...	... ...	huket - ta - ieng - khiuk (*i. e., bring together in one place*).				
Hear ...	arnang ... jang ...	nang	eang	... ...	... ...	ar-'ka-thig-e-le-'the'-kay. (*O.H.B.*) aedie-kă.	
Heart ...	kōi panéweh ...	... ...	elk iumiat; tôt... khugtot (*s*) khau-ghatot. karhû khugtot (*love*). kâag hātôt (*pity*)	... ...	tjerōk.		
Heat ...	heójen ...	... ...	amho-in; hē-ū.				
	tai-en ...	... ...	tanhje.				
Heaven (128 B) ...	(128 B) galahaie	... ...	mioajah. mif houāia.				
Heavy ...	lon-gān ...	... ...	lanient ...	... ...	dā.		
Heel ...	kantol à lá ...	... ...	... ...	... ...	tjœk.		
Helmet ...	ok-hung.						
Hen (129) ...	(129) kamōe ukana.						
Help ...	... ...	... ...	l'hōrmang.				
Here ...	itâ ...	... ...	itâ ...	... ...	o-et ... kowén ...	com-'day. ker'-day. læg-ja da. ker-wen-né-da-kay (*stay here*)	

Hew ...	... ...	... ...	fhâa, reaktsi. tolæt (*hew to pieces*).				
Hiccup ...	hiddau (*Wicks*)	... ...	hehâ.				
Hide (*to h-*) ...	h a m o t h u n g a (*Wicks*).	... ...	hũk.				
High ...	chang dut (*Wicks*)	... ...	kiong ...	... ...	... ...	unchada* ... ella-bot-kay (*high water*). (*O.H.B.*) juru-chaink da (*high tide*).	* A Hindustani word in an Andaman garb (*vide* 'Good.')
Highland ...	... ...	... ...	khui-fô.				
Hill (130) ...	(130) kohinjuan	hombæng ...	... ...	... ...	kosan ...	(*O. H. B.*) bo-runj.	
Hilly ...	tjondet.						
Him ...	... ...	... ...	ané (æ). nhæng, næn.				
Hit ...	haræle (*F. E. T.*) tai-eu.						
Hog ...	nôt ...	... ...	... ...	(*Ham.*) hown ...	man ...	rogo.	
Hold ...	okai (*Wicks*) ...	... ...	... ...	... ...	... ...	ay-ne-kay.	
Hole ...	loka-nang (*hole in the ear*) ...	loñg-ge ...	kæt; lalokeko nang.	... ...	lakaupshe ...	(*O. H. B.*) too-bulleeka.	
Honesty ...	... ...	... ...	lhuh-æhet-atse.				
Honey ...	dhéâgh mat ho-lów-we (*i. e., bees' water*).	... ...	... ...	... ...	... ...	arjar. (*O. H. B.*) agā.	
Hook ...	karau hat lot (*fish-hook*).	... ...	man.				
	kantjap kanhoin (*eye and hook*).	... ...	sanlua.				
Horn ...	hahtaup ...	... ...	sinâah.				

The vowels are sounded as in German or Hindustani; *j* as *y* in 'yard;' *ei* and *ai* are sounded like 'eye;' *au* as in 'Auge;' (German); *æ* as *ai* in 'fair;' *œ* as in 'Oel' (German); *ch* soft as *ch* in 'loch.'

128 *A.—Rosen.* '*Goëh.*'
128 *B.—Rosen.* '*Galahaia.*'

129.—*Fontana.* '*Taffoach;*' *not recognized in the present day by the natives.*
130.—*Fontana.* '*Maude.*'

English Words.	The Nancowry Dialect.	Great Nicobar.	Teressa by M. Plaisant.	Car Nicobar.	Inland Race 'Shobængs.'	Andaman Words.	Remarks.
Horse (131) ...	(131) ghora.						
Hot ...	ke-ó-jen ; tain (*F. E. T.*) (*vide* Heat).	... ...	... ...	... ...	shomhœa ...	on'-yer-da.	
House (132) (133)	(132) gñi ...	... ...	nhjée nji ... tinlap nhjēē (*before the house*)	(133) patti	... ...	tjangda. budelin.	
How	katōm (*how many*). tamenāi ...	... ...	katsi-ka ... omnóan (*how many*). omnan (*how much*).	... ...	tani (*how many*).	(*O. H. B.*) boodhla.	
Human ...	... ...	... ...	nkōnhje (*h—being*)	... ...	kalél.		
Humour ...	... ...	... ...	kinté (*bad h-*)				
Humpback ...	omô ...	... ...	karhû-huk.				
Hundred (134)	tanein inein (*of nuts*). (134) tanein umdjōmé *of other things* (*but of nuts it means 'four hundred'*).	... ...	iangnang. som khinnhi. tanein-umdjomeh.				
Hunger ...	oi-gña ...	go-it ...	honhe ...	(*Gal.*) l'hop ...	patōan ...	akagarikay.	
Hunt ...	... ...	... ...	... ...	... ...	... ...	rogo thellekay (*h- pigs*).	
Hurt ...	... ...	... ...	... ...	... ...	... ...	choom'-da. ardgarreray (*to h-*).	
Husband ...	nkoinje ...	... ...	nkonhje.				
Hut (135) ...	(135) gñi. gni kopula (*beehive formed h-*).						

I.

I ...	tjūa ...	tjuen ...	khiu ...	... ...	itjé ...	dolla; angol. arkawellupkay (*I have done enough*).
Idle ...	hátakeien.					
Idol ...	karéav. karé-a-va.					
If ...	... ...	... ...	ianæ, ianet.			
Ignorant ...	... ...	... ...	hat-liap.			
Illness ...	pomkei-e.					
Illtreat ...	... ...	... ...	holhæhang'n ...	... ...	tain.	
Imitate ...	(*E. H. M.*) hoom-yee (*copy*).	... ...	akhiot-la-mang.			
Immediately ...	... ...	... ...	hetsig'n.			
Immortal ...	... ...	... ...	hat-râatk-kapæt.			
Immoveable ...	... ...	... ...	nphê.			
Impossible ...	(*E. H. M.*) oola-hadsheh.					
Impost ...	... ...	... ...	hat-râatk.			
In ...	... ...	... ...	hâane.			
Incessantly ...	... ...	... ...	hetsig'n.			
Inconstant ...	... ...	... ...	hat-râatk-nphô. hat-râatk-nphé.			
Indecent ...	... ...	... ...	hat-tulau-atse.			
Indefatigable ...	... ...	... ...	hat-râatk-kenhāie.			
Inebriate ...	hujōó ...	... ...	... ...	... ...	kalœv.	
Inform ...	... ...	... ...	... ...	... ...	... ...	(*O. H. B.*) pur-cheka.
Insanity ...	... ...	... ...	pahāl-pâhé.			
Inside ...	al ...	... ...	hâane.			
Instruct ...	... ...	... ...	siap.			

I

The vowels are sounded as in German or Hindustani; *j* as *y* in 'yard;' *ei* and *ai* are sounded like 'eye;' *au* as in 'Auge' (German); *æ* as *ai* in 'fair;' *œ* as in 'Oel' (German); *ch* soft as *ch* in 'loch.'

131.—*Hindustani; this is, perhaps, the last word in the language that has been adopted.*

132.—*Rosen.* '*Njî.*'

133.—*Hamilton.* '*Albanum.*'

134.—*Fontana.* '*Sicom-sicom.*'

135.—*E. H. Man.* '*Kunsherpa,*' (*doubtful*).

English Words.	The Nancowry Dialect.	Great Nicobar.	Teressa by M. Plaisant.	Car Nicobar.	Inland Race 'Shobængs.'	Andaman Words.	Remarks.
Interpreter ...	... ...	... ...	hinhi.				
Invitation ...	(*E. H. M.*) kala kala younde.	... ...	hukèt-vim (*invite*).				
Iron ...	karau ...	kadō ...	garau ...	... ...	nāk ...	(*O. H. B.*) tool-but. wólu.	
Is ...	ôt ...	... ...	... ...	... ...	lāk ...	mieh-'e-bar-da (*what is it ?*)	
Island (136) ...	(136) ohœv ... marty ...	... ...	matahæt. pulo (*Malay*).				
It ...	(*E. H. M.*) an *or* poonan.	... ...	ju tong amé (*it rains*).	... ...	... ...	umé-la-par'-kay (*it rains*). wool-lun-tho-ga-da (*it blows hard*). polour chainkdă (*it is rough*).	
J.							
Jacket ...	kanjut ...	kanhóin.					
Jacktree ...	nankā.						
Jar (137) ...	(137) (*A. C. M.*) oorat.						
Joint ...	... ...	... ...	khinmunté.				
Joke ...	... ...	... ...	huhiaæt.				
Jump (137 A) ...	tinhopshe ...	hamp poi (137A)	... ...	... ...	tjūe ...	ar-kun-thol kay tab-bal-pe-kay	
Jungle (137 B) ...	oltjōa ...	hœvbeñg (137B) kamev alœa.	... ...	... ...	katoñg ...	(*O. H. B.*) ta-lama.	
Just ...	... ...	... ...	tulan.				
K.							
Kanlahe ...	*This is the Nicobar name for the English Settlement.*						

Katchal (*island*)..	Tehnju.					
Keep ...	... ...	... ...	hanhoume ...	... ...	... ...	(*O. H. B.*) tagēēka.
Keg (138) ...	(138) pipe.					
Kettle ...	(*Nov.*) poonhagna.					
Key ...	tenwā ...	... ...	kinmeck ... kinvâi.	(*Gal.*) japi.		
Kidney ...	kanpōng.					
Kill (139) ...	(139) kalok ...	... ...	fââkhni, tamtinlōk.	... ...	olá ...	arb-jer'-rellekay.
	huri tafoa ...	... ...	huhi; tui ...	... ...	... ...	kop-kay.
Kind ...	... ...	... ...	... ...	... ...	... ...	or'-ko-thie-berrin-ga
King conque ...	elcila ...	... ...	... ...	... ...	wó-a.	
King-fisher ...	shâ-a.					
Kiss ...	tong-i-tjé-ra ...	to-i-nan ...	... ...	... ...	ojé ...	orko-loo'-chookay lutj ukay.
Knee ...	kokanoang ...	... ...	kuikanān ...	... ...	... ...	arbloda.
Knife ...	inôt-te-àk ...	... ...	kafai, kaiduma...	... ...	hanat ...	ko'-no-da.
			kanâat te pemetcheu.	... ...	... ...	(*O. H. B.*) koona.
			kirhi.			
Know ...	ăkah; léap ...	... ...	akah; kit-akah (*don't know*).	... ...	nang.	
Knowledge ...	... ...	... ...	liap. ta-liap.			
L.						
Lad ...	iloo; kanjom ...	... ...	... ...	... ...	bagñal.	
Ladder ...	halāk ...	... ...	tahia, tahjâ ...	(*Gal.*) tahiaal; tahja.		

The vowels are sounded as in German or Hindustani; *j* as *y* in 'yard;' *ei* and *ai* are sounded like 'eye;' *au* as in 'Auge' (German); *æ* as *ai* in 'fair;' *œ* as in 'Oel' (German); *ch* soft as *ch* in 'loch.'

136.—*Novara and E. H. Man. 'Poolgna.' This is a corrupt spelling of the Malay word, and it is very curious that it is spelt alike in both these collections.*

137.—*E. H. Man. 'Koodun.'*

137A.—*Wicks. 'Kaupoi.'*

137 B.—*Wicks. 'Hangoee.'*

138.—*From the Portuguese.*

139.—*Galatea 'ud?' Novara 'oorree' ('huri?;') E. H. Man 'thaw kooee?' F. E. T. 'oodee.'*

English Words.	The Nancowry Dialect.	Great Nicobar.	Teressa by M. Plaisant.	Car Nicobar.	Inland race 'Shobængs.'	Andaman Words.	Remarks.
Ladle ...	hanæt deagh ... tajak tjoa. ja shanéal.	... ...	... ...	... ...	tosh.		
Lamb ...	kapéræ tompæn-she.	... ...	khuæn-mhæ. mhæaram.				
Lame ...	she-ka-en ...	... ...	... ...	... ...			
Lamp (140) (141)	gni-he-ō-e ...	thuk autoan (*Wicks*).	khiuk-tamâai ...	(140) sitom tamié.	henlœen ...	ongé-gow-kay.	
Lance ...	(*vide* Spear) ...	... ...	timlok.				
Land (142) ...	(142) lenkí ...	... ...	fō.				
Languti (143) ...	(143) lam-œl.						
Lantern ...	gñi he-ō-e.						
Lard ...	onhéang.						
Large (144) ...	(144) kadū ...	... ...	... ...	... ...	... ...	i-ji-bærigada. thógarda. ro-cho-ba.	
Language ...	(*F. E. T.*) la-ărb.						
Laugh (145) ...	iti ; ité ...	... ...	hiti ...	(145) (*Ham.*) aye-laur.	... ...	yongekay.	
Law ...	... ...	... ...	khiangsé.				
Lay (146) ...	lōm ... pū-jé.	... ...	... ...	... ...	... ...	(*O. H. B.*) bula-geeka.	
Lazy ...	halakei-en.						
Lead (147) ...	(147) hindul (*l-of a ship*). tjomba (*the metal*)	... ...	prata.				
Leaf ...	delœ, tanjām ... otæ, da ugni ... læde méat (*for cigarettes*). akæ, aké (*panleaf*)	... ...	pūron. eang shiâ ; eang khiâ rāe. ...	... ...	... ...	chic-kɛ-da.	
Leak ...	pañg-en-hæ ...	... ...	... ...	... ...	... ...	(*O. H. B.*) ar-toobkă.	
Lean ...	kong-ap-na-shæ..	... ...	ivi kopne.				

Learn ...	... ...	... ...	... ...	... ...	... ...	ic-ke-arb-'kay.
Leather ...	ōk ...	... ...	hūk.			
Leave ...	... ...	... ...	heagn hægn. huh'hæg'n.			
Lecher ...	... ...	... ...	(*vide* Lustful) ...	... ...	... ...	(*vide lustful*).
Leg (148) ...	(148) la karoeit.	... ...	... ...	... ...	... ...	(*O.H.B.*) pāgdă.
Lemon ...	karoeit.					
Lend ...	metām.					
Lessen ...	... ...	... ...	hehetsi. kipsi.			
Lest ...	... ...	... ...	tēn, tīn.			
Let ...	... ...	... ...	... ...	... ...	... ...	mo'-cho-on'-kay (*let us go*).
Letter ...	... ...	... ...	tsi-ghēn.			
Liar ...	paju-te-mitāi.					
Liberate ...	... ...	... ...	huh'hæg'n.			
Lick {	... ...	... ...	... ...	... ...	... ...	poo-loth-kay.
	... ...	... ...	... ...	... ...	... ...	(*O. H. B.*) ur-pul-uch-ka.
Lie ...	lōm (*l-down*) ...	... ...	... ...	... ...	... ...	arth-bul'-ler-ge-kay.
Lie (*untruth*) ...	me-tā-i ...	... ...	min honn'he ...	... ...	... ...	ar-kun-yon-ger-le-kay.
			mitāĕ ...	... ...	... ...	i-djaj-kay.
Life ...	(*E. H. M.*) ahn	... ...	hæng.			
Lifeless ...	kapá.					
Lift ...	o-e-té wa ...	... ...	hukét hukiét.			
Light (149) ...	hat-loñg-an (*not heavy*).	... ...	akapset (*light a fire*).	... ...	... ...	cha-rug-da.
	(149) ning mait (*a light*).	... ...	pœ (*clearness*) ...	... ...	... ...	(*O. H. B.*) surum.

The vowels are sounded as in German or Hindustani; *j* as *y* in 'yard;' *ei* and *ai* are sounded like 'eye'; *au* as in 'Auge' (German); *ae* as *ai* in 'fair;' *œ* as in 'Oel' (German); *ch* soft as *ch* in 'loch.'

140.—*Car Nicobar, Gal.*, '*dhink foltene.*'
141.—*Schowra., deRff.*, '*balaé.*'
142.—*Novara.* '*Oal mattai*' (*so also E. H. Man*).
143.—*The strip of cloth which the men wear.*
144.—*Novara.* '*Kadoo,*' (*so also E. H. Man*).
145.—*Car Nicobar, Gal.*, '*ajelkue.*'
146.—*Schowra. deRff.*, '*pòshe.*'
147.—*Fontana.* '*Luva.*'
148.—*Fontana* 1795, '*hanhan;*' *Barbe* 1847, '*anhnan.*'
149.—*E. H. M.* '*Hai yooing*' (*light a fire*).

English Words.	The Nancowry Dialect.	Great Nicobar.	Teressa by M. Plaisant.	Car Nicobar.	Inland race 'Shobængs.'	Andaman words.	Remarks.
Lightning (150)	(150)(*Novara*)mait	... ...	meïk.				
Like (151) ...	(151) jondo ...	... ...	heng halâal. tsie; vetseng.				
Lime (152) (153)	shun (*quick l.*) karoeit(*the fruit*). (152) karoeitsho-kap (*little l-*).	... ...	... ...	namma ...	tjil.		
Limp ...	she-æ-un.						
Line ...	fanué (*string*).						
Linen ...	loé		akhik (*wash l.*) loæ.				
Lip ...	mano-in ...	... ...	menua ...	... ...	pano-i ...	orkopaida.	
Liquor ...	wiìnjc ...	... ...	kanhoing. tarām.				
Listen ...	arnang ...	... ...	eng.				
Little ...	tompænshe ...	... ...	peit æt ... pi metscheu ...	... ...	tjó-ang-ko-e	arkit jada. kitie-mada. (*O. H. B.*) kiteama.	
Live ...	... ...	... ...	hæng; nphô ...	... ...	... ...	par-le'-kay.	
Living ...	(*Nov.*) ahn.						
Liver ...	... ...	... ...	halep; ntap ...	... ...	... ...	djiri.	
Lizard ...	koa ...	... ...	... ...	... ...	... ...	tatte marda.	
Loin ...	do-an-ge ...	ku-dañg-ge.					
Long ...	tiram (*l-ago*) ...	... ...	... ...	... ...	kæ-e-mo (*long time*).	(*O. H. B.*) ur-tām (*l-ago*).	
	di-utten; hœ-i (*far*).	... ...	... ...	... ...	gna-e-kœ (*far*)		
Look ...	haró-é (*l-at*) ...	... ...	harea ... hahea ...	... ...	mæ-mæ-te-kœ	ichburthekay. (*O. H. B.*) ar-lōōka.	
Looking-glass ...	tingmælæ ... tingmæalæ.	... ...	tèn mela.				
London ...	Lano akæ (*i. e., betel-crusher*) *the name of a chief at Itoe.*						

Lose ...	eja ...	... ...	heâgn ; hægn.			
Loudly ...	... ...	... ...	... ...	... ...	... ...	(*O. H. B.*) pa-kēēka (*call out l-*).
Love ...	(*Nov.*) soojonghien	... ...	karhû kbugtot kâaghôt-hâhi-tin.	... ...	... ...	orkojangekay.
Lovely ...	... ...	... ...	kuchi ki.			
Low ...	... ...	... ...	hurōh ...	... ...	... ...	ellaairkay (*l- water*). (*O. H. B.*) ula-irkă.
Lukewarm ...	taiñg ahe ...	... ...	akahe ...	... ...	shom hœ.	
Lustful ...	... ...	... ...	lang ...	... ...	... ...	djerri djobda. doruda ladj kay.
M.						
Mackerel fish ...	sa-jó.					
Magician (154) ...	(154) manlōene	panloene ...	... ...	... ...	ajov.	
Maiden ...	kanjōm enkāna	ogñjæ-ojœhe ...	... ...	... ...	a diuk.	
Mainland ...	... ...	... ...	matāhæt-te-Karhû	... ...	ojœ ta de en.	
Maize ...	kolonáte.					
Make ...	momi ...	... ...	huhé ; huhomi	... ...	... ...	tappeek-kay. (*O. H. B.*) ool-ōōka.
			kun-vi ; ...	... ...	... ...	arkunggoo rookay (*m- a noise*).
			kunhuhomi ; te vi vihuk ; vi-khiuk-haheng (*m- room*). akhik (*m- white*). athuak (*m- black*).			

The vowels are sounded as in German or Hindustani; *j* as *y* in 'yard;' *ei* and *ai* are sounded like 'eye;' *au* as in 'Auge' (German); *æ* as *ai* in 'fair;' *œ* as in 'Oel' (German); *ch* soft as *ch* in 'loch.'

150.—*E. H. M.* '*Maig.*'
151.—*E. H. M.* '*Hang nesheh*' (*doubtful*).
152.—*Rosen.* '*Sukâk.*'
153.—*Schowra., deRff.,* '*shokāko.*'

154.—*These magicians or priests pretend to be able to cure all diseases and pretend to fight the spirits on all occasions. They practise as jugglers and, I believe, a little in ventriloquism. They have, however, no power, as has lately been suggested.*

English Words.	The Nancowry Dialect.	Great Nicobar.	Teressa by M. Plaisant.	Car Nicobar.	Inland race 'Shobængs.'	Andaman Words.	Remarks.
Malady ...	pomkcie ...	fo-ap ...	... ...		o-egn-ehæ. o-e-he.		
Malay (155) ...	(155) paju shom malāju.						
Male ...	nkonje.						
Man (156) (156A)	(156) paju (*Nicobarian*).	otœhe ...	baju; pahé ...	(*Ham*). kegonia...	vadue ...	(*O.H.B.*) aboola.	
	eukōnje (*male*) (156A).	... ...	nkonhje (*husband*)	... ...	... ...	(*O.H.B.*) abara. (*unmarried*).	
	joang (*some one*)	... ...	râmé pahé (*every one*).				
	kalein (*foreigner*)	... ...	kaiet ...	... ...	... ...	(*O.H.B.*) abchabil (*married*).	
	maial (*youth*) ...	... ...	sum (*people*).				
	pomoœshé (*old man*).						
	ilōō (*bachelor*).						
	paju te ita (*Nancowry man.*)						
	pu (*Car Nicobarian*).						
	tatăt (*man from Schowra*).						
	loang (*Coast-man from Great Nicobars*).						
	shobæng (*aborigines at Great Nicobars*).						
	tjong hinkok (*man of war*).						
Man-catcher ...	hetnât ...	pandol.					
Many	orohætse; hurohetse.	bishe ...	... ...	... ...	gœt.		
	hoœ; tjoha.	... ...	... ...	... ...	tani (*how m.*)		
	katom (*how m—*)						
	tamanai (*how m—*)						

Marble (157) ...	... ...	... ...	(157)patu-ta-lopāh			
Married ...	enjūle ...	ōmi ...	... ...	... ...	kamiak ...	(O. H. B.) adaneekâ.
Massacre ...	tjak kapá ...	tap-po ...	... ...	(Gal). kiattra-i.		
Mast ...	hintæhæ ...	hintæhæ ...	... ...	... ...	lœ-nam-dœ.	
Mat (158) ...	(158) hilaok ...	hilœ-e ...	nkō hitiak ... (bast to sleep on).	... ...	akoeit.	
Matches ...	mané heō-e antas heō-e. ...	vanō-hintán.				
Matter ...	... ...	... ...	lahuhōt (pus).			
Me ...	tju ; tjue ...	tjun.				
Meagre ...	... ...	... ...	ivi kopne (become m—)			
Meaning ...	... ...	... ...	tsie ghēn.			
Measure, (159) ...	(159) idi ; harrow	... ...	haraak.			
Meat ...	... ...	... ...	hæng.			
Medicine ...	lanūn ...	danún ...	renâant ...	... ...	dañg.	
Megapodius, (Nicobaricus).	mæ-ké-en ...	katjav ...	... ...	... ...	akoeit.	
Melancholy ...	... ...	... ...	kistot.			
Melon ...	tamikāē.					
Menstruation ...	mahām ...	tjoñg-ha ...	... ...	... ...	adait.	
Merchandize ...	... ...	... ...	iak. kinhji.			
Merchant ...	... ...	... ...	patre-ta-kinhji.			
Metal ...	... ...	... ...	hēhang.			
Midday ...	kamheng ...	kaphein.				
Middle ...	... ...	... ...	milæt. nchōŭč.			
Midnight ...	yuang hatam ...	tāme ...	... ...	... ...	ke-ein.	
Milk ...	gñjo ...	... ...	manam ...	... ...	wu-i-po ...	ulitj-kay. (O. H. B.) raj.
Milt ...	ehó-aje.					

The vowels are sounded as in German or Hindustani; *j* as *y* in 'yard'; *ei* and *ai* are sounded like 'eye;' *au* as in 'Auge' (German); *æ* as *ai* in 'fair;' *œ* as in 'Oel' (German); *ch* soft as *ch* in 'loch.'

155.—*Novara.* '*Kolog-hamatt,*' *yellow man. Very doubtful.*
156.—*Rosen.* '*Djin-baju*' (*man*); '*umjáha*' (*old man*); '*eloh*' (*yôuth*).
156 A.—*F. E. T.* '*Commansi.*'
157.—*This is a very doubtful expression. It means 'good stone.'*
158. *Hænsel.* '*Hetfat.*'
159.—*E. H. Man.* '*Tah.*'

English Words.	The Nancowry dialect.	Great Nicobar.	Teressa by M. Plaisant.	Car Nicobar.	Inland race 'Shobængs.'	Andaman words.	Remarks.
Mina (*Eulabes Andamanensis.*)	(*Rosen.*) ganjaú.						
Mind ...	kahatoaré (*never m—*) watme njañgga to (*never m—*)	nga-na-ha-au-ré... (*never m—*)	... ...	... ...	tjomga (*never m—*)		
Minor ...	kanjom ilō ...	omieñg.					
Mirror ...	tingmæélch ...	tamealeh.					
Miserly ...	... ...	... ...	kalet.				
Miss (*with a gun*) (159A.)	(*F. E. T.*) (159A) ha-tai-eu.						
Misuse ...	... ...	... ...	holhæhang'n.				
Mix ...	ka-law-we ...	gña kashœme ...	... ...	... ...	gœ-bo-i-hing.		
Mob ...	... ...	... ...	luluh't.				
Moist ...	... ...	... ...	vi hanâi-khui (*moisten*). vi-haming (*moisten*). pahia.				
Money ...	rupej (*rupee*) ... para (*Mexican dollar*).	ada (*Mexican dollar*).					
Monkey (160) ...	ke-in ... doæng.	pajun ...	kaiing; kejin ...	... ...	tjoit.		
Monsoon ...	haé fol (*N. E. Monsoon*). shohong (*S. W. Monsoon*).	kajœl fōl (*N. E. M.*) kajœl shinhoang-ga (*S. W. M.*)					
Month ...	kahæ (*i. e., moon*)	... ...	... ...	... ...	hov-up.		
Monthly ...	kahæ te kahæ ...	... ...	... ...	(*Gal.*) tingæt.			
Moon (161) ...	(161) kahæ ...	... ...	manâat (*new m—*) renaang (*full m—*).	... ...	... ...	o-goorda.	
More ...	pa-i-te-ræ ...	... ...	hēhăne.				

Morning ...	al haki (*sunrise*)	ja-bœ ...	aki ...	... ...	wallahæ ...	(*O. H. B.*) ul-waka.
	kohin doáha (*fore-noon*).	... ...	næn-aki (*this m—*)			
Mortal ...	... ...	... ...	râatk-kapæt.			
Mosquito ...	mihoja ...	bishoæñg ...	... ...	... ...	bo-et.	
Mother ...	tjia enkana (*woman parent*).	heen ...	iæie ...	... ...	de-it ...	arbæteræ; tsha-nola.
			ten ...	... ...	... ...	char'-nar; ma-mola.
Mother-in-law ...	komjan.					
Move	... ...	... ...	he gn (hægn) ...	... ...	... ...	o'-cho-thoon (*m—up or down*).
	... ...	... ...	kunbæhic.			
	... ...	... ...	kutuhæ, huh'-hæg'n.			
Mount ...	kohinjuan ...	koshit ...	khui-fô ...	... ...	shat.	
Mouse ...	kom-æt ...	komshæñg ...	kum't ...	... ...	aki-it ...	rogoo-tart'-ma.
Mouth (162) (163)	(162) olfang ...	... ...	monoi ...	... ...	hilœk fakse ...	ar-ka-bung-da.
	ahœl ...	... ...	imiang kinluehsi (*one m-full*).	... ...	... ...	mi-ti-tog-da.
Much ...	hurōhatse ...	bīshe ...	karhûatse (*too m—*)	... ...	gœt ...	(*O. H. B.*) ki-teama (*not m—*)
	kadu ...	... ...	hchōr; harohatse			
	pahū-e.					
Mud ...	... ...	... ...	... ...	... ...	.. ..	(*O. H. B.*) gara.
Murder (164) (164 A.)	(164) huri tafoa	tappo (164A) ...	fhâa khui.			
			tam tinlok.			
Muscle ...	(*E. H. M.*) e-hay	unfoi (*Wicks*) ...	haheang.			
Musket ...	hindæl ...	tinfói ...	... ...	... ...	fuñg (*i.e., cross-bow*).	
Mussel (*bivalve*)	héev.					
	hagñei.					
Mustachle ...	enjōm ...	kanoñp ...	... ...	... ...	behol.	
Mute ...	... ...	... ...	hat nheōle.			

The vowels are sounded as in German or Hindustani; *j* as *y* in 'yard;' *ei* and *ai* are sounded like 'eye;' *au* as in 'Auge' (German); *æ* as *ai* in 'fair;' *œ* as in 'Oel' (German); *ch* soft as *ch* in 'loch.'

159A.—*Vide* 111*A*, *vide* Hit.
160.—*Katchall, deRff.*, '*morangshe.*'
161.—*Rosen.* '*Ghahœ.*'
162.—*Gal.* '*meno;*' *Nov.* '*manoing.*' *Rosen.* '*manóing;*' *vide also the Teressa column and* 163. *I believe, though I have so many authorities against me, that* '*manoing*' *means lip or lips and not mouth. F. E. T. mănōin. Compare furthermore* Lip *in the Teressa column.*
163.—*Schowra, Gal.*, '*manoing;*' *vide* 162.
164.—*E. H. Man.* '*Thaw-kooee?*'
164A.—*Wicks.* '*Taffo.*'

English Words.	The Nancowry dialect.	Great Nicobar.	Teressa by M. Plaisant.	Car Nicobar.	Inland race 'Shobængs.'	Andaman words.	Remarks.
Muzzle (*of a gun*)	olmó ahan.						
My (165) (*mine-myself*).	(165) tjué ...	tjun ...	kahihot (*my friend*). khin (*I, my, mine*). tsang kji.				
N.							
Nail (166) (*of finger*).	kishoa ...	kisho ...	kissot ...	(*Gal.*) ginsa ...	agib ...	tol-boat. mo-id-bo-do.	
	kishoja ...	... ...	... ...	... ...	... ...	(*O. H. B.*) bood-da.	
Nail (*of iron*) ...	hinæm.						
Naked ...	oltjal.						
Name ...	léang ...	... ...	... ...	... ...	mænde— d j œ-m æ-m æ (*what is the n.*)		
Nancowry ...	se-pi-pe.						
Nasty (166A) ...	hat lapoó ...	op-ak (166A) ...	... ...	... ...	œk-œ.		
Native ...	paju.						
Nature ...	... ...	... ...	la en taat (*natural*). tsi (*nature*). ta-en-tôt (*naturally*).				
Navel ...	fuhon ...	... ...	fuhōn ...	(*Gal.*) fun ...	kanv.		
Nautilus-shell ...	tama ...	... ...	... ...	... ...	... ...	o'-do-da.	
Nay ...	ha-a.						
Near (166B) ...	me-æ-ho ...	æ-tœ (166B) ...	hemæn ... hat-hâai (*near by*).	... ...	ha-ev ...	(*O.H.B.*) lageea. ar-ka-or-ma.	
Neck ...	un-lon-ge ko-la-la. ...	gna (*Wicks*) ...	nlông ...	(*Gal.*) kilap ...	gnu-en.		
Necklace ...	nient malau tanol ol kolala (*n-tie*). ...	paloo (*Wicks*) ...	molâat ...	(*Gal.*) huhiôat...	shinlō-cit.		

Need ...	jo tôt (*I want*)...	oh-ow (*Wicks*) ...	... ...	... ...	ho-au.	
Needle (167) ...	(167) { tjsadum tjarum.	chadup (*Wicks*)	kiarum ...	... ...	atœm.	
Needless ...	ti tjo ...	... ...	... ...	... ...	na-hō-e.	
Negative ...	... ...	... ...	... ...	... ...	... ...	(*O.H.B.*) yāt da.
Neither ...	... ...	... ...	næt.			
Nephew ...	ha-ó ...	... ...	khuan-eonang ...	... ...	gni-en-tjé.	
Nest (168) ...	hat leit ... (168) hikaé (*eatable bird's n.*)	won (*Wicks*) ...	khæt ...	... ...	... ...	ar-bar-rar-tar-da.
Net ...	(*Wicks*) won ...	(*Wicks*) won ...	... ...	... ...	... ...	coo-da.
Never ...	(*E. H. M.*) kitma	... ...	hatlēt; atavetsen	... ...	gñañg-a-dokle (*n- mind*).	
	kahato aré(*n-mind*)	... ...	hatmanghnhagn. letng.			
New ...	... ...	... ...	manâat (*n- moon*).			
Next ...	seju (*n-time*) ...	jæk ...	... ...	... ...	ijākæ.	
Nice (168A) ...	lapoe (*good*) ...	shæ-i to (168A)...	... ...	... ...	œk-œ ...	(*O.H.B.*) baree gudda.
	shéang (*sweet*).					
Nicobarian ...	paju (*or* ol) de ita (*Nancowry man*). pu (*from Car Nicobar*). tatăt (*Schowra, Teressa*). loang (*coast people at Great Nicobar*). shobæng (*jungle people at the same island*).					

The vowels are sounded as in German or Hindustani; *j* as *y* in 'yard;' *ei* and *ai* are sounded like 'eye;' *au* as in 'Auge' (German); *æ* as *ai* in 'fair;' *œ* as in 'Oel' (German); *ch* soft as *ch* in 'loch.'

165.—*E. H. M.* '*Tchiang chier?*'
166.—*Schowra, de Rff.*, '*kinōt.*'
166*A*.—*Wicks.* '*Oo-buk.*'
166*B*.—*Wicks.* '*Faām.*'

167.—*Malay.*
168.—*Rosen.* '*Egai*' (*eatable bird's nests*).
168*A*.—*Wicks.* '*Polakul.*'

English Words.	The Nancowry dialect.	Great Nicobar.	Teressa by M. Plaisant.	Car Nicobar.	Inland race 'Shobængs.'	Andaman Words.	Remarks.
Niece ...	haé ...	... ...	khuan-eonang. eonang-nkênhje.				
Nigh ...	me æ-ho ...	fæm ?					
Night ...	hatam (*night*). shupheng (*sunset*). ladicjé (*dusk*). pujué (7 *p. m.*) engshe heam auk nôk (8 *p. m.*) heam auk nôk ka (9 *p. m.*) heam auk nôk kejau (10 *p. m.*) engshe joang hatam (11 *p. m.*) joang hatam (12 *night*). hahohaka kajau (1 *a. m.*) hahohakakajauka (3 *a. m.*) puju (5 *a. m.*) tjangiol (*daybreak*).	tamhe ...	atam ...	... ...	ke-ein ...	el-la-ruth-kay. (*O. H. B.*) goo-rūb.	
Nightcap (168B)	karebushe (168B)	sindol (*Wicks*).					
Nine ...	héanghata ... fuan tafuel heang noang tak.	... ...	... ...	(*Gal.*) kinteræ...	nog-in.		
Nineteen ...	shom-héang-hata héang hata tafuel héang noang tak						
Ninety ...	fuan umdjome ruktei. fuan inein tanein tafuel.						

Nipa ...	(*Rosen*) juáng-etuah.						
Nipple ...	tha (*of breast*) ... kanap koihindæl (*of a gun*).	toa (*Wicks*) ...	... ...	... ...	toān.		
No ...	ha-a; hat ... wat ...	gnaho (*Wicks*)...	hat hæn (*not this*)	(*Gal.*) rava	gño-hakæ	yar-bar-da.	
Noise ...	... ...	... ...	... ...	... ...	... ...	(*O.H.B.*) yatda arkungoo'-roo-kay (*to make a n.*) ...	
Nonsense ...	... ...	... ...	mineole (*nonsensical man*).	... ...	... ...	... ...	gairtack.
Noon ...	kamheng ...	kap hein ...	... ...	... ...	ko-kam-kein.		
North (169) ...	(169) kapá ... haéfūl (*N. E. Monsoon*).	kapá (*Wicks*)	lafôr (*N.*) langhapa (*N. W.*)				
Nose (170) ...	(170) gmoa ...	umho ...	mhang ...	(*Gal.*) ehelme ...	monk ...	tjo-ro-ga-da ... chor-ron-gar'-da. tsho-run-ga-da. (*O.H.B.*) choo-roogudda.	I have given four spellings as I have got them from four different sides, just to show how differently people spell the words.
Nosegay ...	... ...	... ...	libré.				
Nostril ...	... ...	... ...	hamôn.				
Not ...	hat; watshe; watme. wat ... tjit akah (*I do n-know*).	gnagnœhitjœ	hat; hathæn (*n-this*). kit akah (*I do not know*).	(*Gal.*) rava	unāng	(*O. H. B.*) lage-ēa (*n-far*). (*O.H.B.*) kitea-mă (*n-much*).	
Nothing ...	hat ôt (*i. e., is not*) gnuñg (*i. e., empty*).	læt ...	hahâat ...	... ...	onheang.		
Nourishment ...	auk nôk ...	... ...	hatnâak.				

The vowels are sounded as in German or Hindustani; *j* as *y* in 'yard;' *ei* and *ai* are sounded like 'eye;' *au* as in 'Auge' (German); *æ* as *ai* in 'fair;' *œ* as in 'Oel' (German); *ch* soft as *ch* in 'loch.'

168C.—*Wicks*, '*kanæala (?)*'; *it means, I believe, "pillow."*
169.—*Rosen.* '*Kofoâ.*'
170.—*Rosen.* '*Moáh.*'

English Words.	The Nancowry Dialect.	Great Nicobar.	Teressa by M. Plaisant.	Car Nicobar.	Inland race 'Shobængs.'	Andaman Words.	Remarks.
Now ...	teja ...	tafem (*Wicks*)	... ...	... ...	... ...	(*O. H. B.*) go-ē-lin.	
Nudity ...	oltjal ...	oolyala (*Wicks*).					
Nurse ...	... ...	... ...	nkênhje-manam. (*wetnurse*).				
O.							
Oar ...	kagnôt / canôt } (*of a European boat*). kajal (*paddle*) ...	kagnôt / canôt } (*Wicks.*) paooa (*Wicks*).	kaheha; pa-i-ju ruhen.	... ...	... ...	(*O. H. B.*) wale-emā.	
Obey ...	(*E.H.M.*) yuyung	... ...	atmi kiha-i.				
Observe ...	... ...	... ...	vi-ta-tsie.				
Obtain ...	... ...	... ...	hâa.				
Ocean ...	kammélæ ...	au (*Wicks*)	nlānhje; nliôn... kamamlæ.	(*Gal.*) mae ...	lōp.		
Occasion ...	... ...	... ...	iana. ianet.				
Occupy ...	... ...	... ...	vihuk.				
Octopus ...	koash. tanaugnat.						
Off ...	ju tju (*I am off*)	... ...	... ...	... ...	... ...	goo-thoo-kay.	
Offend ...	... ...	... ...	hat-tulan-tēn-pâhé.				
Offspring ...	nkonje ...	... ...	... ...	... ...	kœ-tjœ.		
Often ...	(*E. H. M.*) dull.						
Oh ...	... ...	... ...	la.				
Oil ...	gñait ...	gna (*Wicks*)	māik'ē ...	(*Gal.*) eahve.			
Omit ...	pæñg-na-to ...	... ...	fuongato.				
Old ...	pomó æshe ...	ong sheong (*Wicks*).	kaiet; kaviēt ...	... ...	... ...	etar'larteemda.	
On (171) ...	latshi ... (171) knallen (*on high*).	... ...	mhænhje; tschi hafot sang'n (*go on board*). khui.	... ...	... ...	patada lāpana?	

One ...	héang ...	... ...	sa (*once* ;) iang ; nan. kua, ki, kâa (*one another*).	... ...	... ...	ob-boo-bo-thool'da.
Onion (172) (173)	(172) powang ...	powang (*Wicks*) (172.)	(173) sabola.			
Open (174) ...	(174) kawáhigne	woje ...	fôlt ...	... ...	wœnde.	
Opening ...	... ...	... ...	keātatû.			
Oppose ...	... ...	... ...	hatalāng.			
Or ...	... ...	... ...	hat khiuk-khiuka (*either——or*).			
Orange ...	karoeit shéang ...	oomtiang (*Wicks*)	kamang-kalin ...	(*Gal.*) peku ...	karoigne.	
Order ..	... ...	... ...	ivihoatse ; hehot.			
Organ ...	... ...	... ...	kalhahōt (*pubes*).			
Oriel ...	tjélau.		ka-huhiaæt.			
Ornament ...	itjé (*ear o-*)	... ...	kinp (*l*) ōng-nang (*ear o-*)			
Orphan ...	... ...	... ...	kapæt-iæt.			
Other ...	... ...	... ...	nreng'n tsie (*something else*).			
Over (171) ...	knallen (171) ...	... ...	hokté. khui.			
Overarm 175 ...	tjanpāk ...	kol.				
Our ...	tjantjéa ...	... ...	hin hing. khinhe.			
Out ...	... ...	... ...	... ...	... ...	... ...	(*O. H. B.*) pa-keeka (*call out loudly*).
Outside ...	... ...	... ...	la hûk ...	... ...	... ...	the-tho'-er-thic-kay.
Oyster ...	sipôt ... kawia ...	kamoñgke ... omshonvve.	... ...	... ...	wēl ; wōt ...	childa.

The vowels are sounded as in German or Hindustani ; *j* as *y* in 'yard ;' *ei* and *ai* sounded like 'eye ;' *au* as in 'Auge' (German) ; *æ* as *ai* in 'fair ;' *œ* as in 'Oel' (German) ; *ch* soft as *ch* in 'loch.'

171.—'*Knallen*' *is a religious expression and is used for the top of every-thing or for* '*over*' *by the priests.*

172.—*Malay.*

173.—*Portuguese.*

174.—*E. H. M.*, '*phoigna.*' *F. E. T.*, '*o-foi.*'

175.—*Schowra, deRff.*, '*nōi,*'

English Words.	The Nancowry dialect.	Great Nicobar.	Teressa by M. Plaisant.	Car Nicobar.	Inland race 'Shobængs.'	Andaman Words.	Remarks.
P.							
Packet ...	... ...	... ...	laming.				
Paddle (176) ...	(176) kajal ... duinde (*to p-*)	ba-o-a ...	... ...	... ...	akoei.		
Padlock ...	tinwa.						
Pail ...	(*Gal.*) hasno-i.						
Pain ...	tjok ...	... ...	khiak ...	... ...	... ...	jo-do-le-churm'-kay.	
Paint ...	lanun (*i. e., medicine*).	danun.					
Pair ...	tafuél (*which also means 'six'*).						
Palm (*of hand*) ...	... ...	... ...	ho kti.				
Palm-wine ...	tóak. ...						
Pampel-moss ...	... ...	... ...	kinvâh.				
Panleaf (*Chavica*) (177) ...	aké ...	panō-o ...	... ...	lakaitje.			
Pandanus (178) (178A).	larôme (*the eatable sort*). hikæ (*the wild sort*).	bœe (178A) ...	... ...	hinfōn (*the eatable sort*).			
Pane ...	tanóang ...	popang (*Wicks*).					
Pantaloons (179)	kanhá ...	kanha (*Wicks*).					
Papaja, (*Carica papaya*).	(*Rosen*) maágh.						
Paper ...	lépré ...	lépré (*Wicks*).					
Parasol ...	... ...	... ...	nron-khui.				
Parent ...	tjia.						
Parrot (180) ...	(180) katōk ...	kantang (*Wicks*)	karaka.				
Partner ...	... ...	... ...	huleang.				
Paste ...	... ...	... ...	harhēha (*p—up*).				
Path (180A) ...	gadji (180 A) ...	kiyoa (*Wicks*) ...	khiâ ...	... ...	... ...	(*O.H.B.*) tinga.	
Pay ...	ha-ju-a-ha ...	... ...	(*deRff.*) hathangh-ah.				

Peal ...	... ...	... ...	peâ.			
Pearl ...	... ...	... ...	... ...	(*Gal.*) tavaate.		
Peel ...	... ...	... ...	hatenk.			
Pen ...	anét lébré ...	anét lébré (*Wicks*).				
Penis ...	lam ...	lub (*Wicks*)	... ...	... ...	... ...	tjulda.
Penitence ...	... ...	anān.				
People ...	paju ...	pău (*Wicks*) ...	sum.			
Pepper (181) ...	(181) larâ ...	larâ (*Wicks*) (181)	kunmenta.			
Perceive ...	haio (*Wicks*) ...	haio (*Wicks*) ...	... ...	... ...	... ...	(*O. H. B.*) ar-loōkă.
Perhaps ...	jong-hareh ...	... ...	hat sak'n.			
Perish ...	kapa ...	kapæ tji ...	hahabram.			
Perspiration ...	hoáng ...	tanet kumat.				
Petticoat ...	ok jok loé enkana.					
Physic ...	lánūn.					
Physician ...	manlóene.					
Piety ...	... ...	... ...	kâag'hâtōt.			
Pig (182) (183A)	(182) nôt ...	bakoi ...	(*deRff.*) kavoake	(183A.) (*Ham.*) hown.	noñg ...	rogoo.
	sharúal (*wild p*—)	tjong (*wild p*—)	... ...	... ...	alœv (*wild p-*).	
Pig-spear ...	*a.*—haploap ...	*a.*—jué.				
	b.—hom i-j a-ter (*old-fashioned, made of iron, from Schowra*).	*b.*—kadoa tom-téin.	... ...	... ...	*b.*—ado.	
	c.—mon heang (*with one barbe*).					
	d.—shanein jeno-ma (*with two barbes*).	*d.*—ahin.				

The vowels are sounded as in German or Hindustani; *j* as *y* in 'yard;' *ei* and *ai* are sounded like 'eye;' *au* as in 'Auge' (German); *æ* as *ai* in 'fair;' *œ* as in 'Oel (German); *ch* soft as *ch* in 'loch.'

176.—*E. H. Man.* '*Pow wha.*'
177.—*Schowra, deRff.*, '*hijū.*'
178.—*Rosen.* '*Larôm.*'
178*A*.—*Wicks.* '*Boana.*'
179.—*Schowra, deRff.*, '*henjōt.*'

180.—*Rosen.* '*Katáagh.*'
180 *A*.—*Wicks* '*Kiyee.*'
181.—*Malay.*
182.—*Rosen.* '*Nôt.*'
183 *A*.—*Gal.* '*Kahuhoke.*'

English Words.	The Nancowry dialect.	Great Nicobar.	Teressa by M. Plaisant.	Car Nicobar.	Inland race 'Shobængs.'	Andaman Words.	Remarks.
Pigeon (183B) ...	*a.*—mūmū (*Carpophaga sylvatica v. ænea*) imperial.	*a.*—kaél.					
	b.—kajœl (*Carpophaga bicolor*) white.						
	c.—ok to agh (*Macropygia rufipennis*) red dove.	*c.*—ogdoaka.					
	d.—n-ka-lau (*Calænas nicobaricus*) Nicobar pigeon.	*d.*—nōng ...	... ...	... ...	*d*—adūa.		
	e.—kahouk (*Janthænas palum-boides*) red-eyed imperial.	*e.*—kahouk.					
	f.—tomoa (*Chalcophaps indicus*) ordinary dove.	... ...	kahaak (*dove*).				
	g.—kapak (*Osmotreron chloroptera*) green pigeon.	*g.*—kapak.					
Pillow ...	kanéla ...	... ...	kanihēle-khui ...	... ...	damkoi.		
Pin ...	itji.						
Pinch ...	njim hata ...	... ...	... ...	... ...	... ...	arb-top'-pe-kay.	
Pineapple (184) (185).	(184) shurû ...	shuta ...	fûrong ...	(*Ham.*) frung. ...	bu-e-læk.		
Pipe ...	tanop.						
Pisang ...	... ...	... ...	hibuga.				

Pity ...	... ...	... ...	kâag hâtot.				
Place ...	... ...	... ...	khiuk ... khiuk khiniong (*anchorage*).	... ...	... ...	(*O. H. B*) aēr (*i. e., place of rest*).	
Plant ...	op-æp (*to pl—*)	... ...	h (*k*) adep! hēp (*to pl-*)				
Plantain ...	hibu ...	shoat ...	hibô ... kuluam.	tanjo gua ...	mun ...	angragadda*...	* This must be a new word, for the fruit was introduced into the Settlement.
Plaster ...	... ...	... ...	renâant.				
Plate ...	pitéeng.						
Play ...	danôn (*on a musical instrument*).	... ...	... ...	... ...	... ...	me-jarj-kay (*as children*).	
Plenty ...	urohatse ...	... ...	... ...	... ...	... ...	(*O. H. B.*) cha-nukda.	
Pocket ...	kanho.						
Pocket handkerchief.	tanot hoang ...	tanet enmat.					
Podex ...	... ...	... ...	... ...	... ...	... ...	(*O. H. B.*) da-mada.	
Point ...	... ...	... ...	nēne (*p- out*) ...	... ...	... ...	onko-thig-row-kay.	
Pointed ...	... ...	... ...	hituhaman.				
Pony (186) ...	(186) ghora.						
Population ...	(*Gal.*) goæh? ...	... ...	khui.				
Poor ...	poap ... lom ...	... ...	hathû l'hôm. kihâe.				
Porpoise ...	ka-po-ang.						
Possess ...	... ...	... ...	khjiang.				
Possible ...	... ...	... ...	râatk-ivi.				
Pot (187) ...	(187) ashōi ...	igna ...	... ...	... ...	awœk.		
Potatoe ...	kobæng (*yams*)...	... ...	kuping-kalin (*sweet p-*)				

The vowels are sounded as in German or Hindustani; *j* as *y* in 'yard;' *ei* and *ai* are sounded like 'eye;' *au* as in 'Auge' (German); *æ* as *ai* in 'fair,' *œ* as in 'Oel' (German); *ch* soft as *ch* in 'loch.'

183 *B.—The bird marked* (*e.*) *is a new bird. It was first brought to Europe by the writer, first described by Mr. Hume, the great Indian authority on birds.*

184.—*Rosen.* '*Sudú.*' *F. E. T.* '*suru;*' *both pronunciations are correct in their way.*

185.—*Schowra, de Rff.,* '*funung.*'

186.—*Hindustani.*

187.—*Gal.* '*Hashoi,*' '*kurian,*' '*karian;*' *the latter are doubtful words.*

English Words.	The Nancowry Dialect.	Great Nicobar.	Teressa by M. Plaisant.	Car Nicobar.	Inland race 'Shobængs.'	Andaman Words.	Remarks.
Pour ...	tamló ...	... ...	fuhotet; kumonk-let. kuvé.				
Prawn ...	shoang ...	dah ...	... ...	... ...	bo-it.		
Precious ...	... ...	... ...	kuchi ki.				
Pregnant ...	komhosh kanjom	kadōje ...	hehumé hæhokre (*make pr-*)	... ...	kœthokaun ...	arbodida.	
Prepare ...	... ...	... ...	hâ.				
Present ...	tanialshe (*gift*)...	... ...	nēu-maka (*pr- at*)	(*Gal.*) tahæi (*pr- at*).	jo-i-tæ-tjé (*a pr-*)	(*O. H. B.*) go-é-lin.	
Press ...	... ...	... ...	nlen.				
Pretend ...	... ...	... ...	metām.				
Pretty (188) ...	(188) lapoé ...	kœ ...	lopat-makmet ...	... ...	o-o.		
Price ...	... ...	... ...	hahehaæng. hathahang'n.				
Priest ...	manlóene ...	... ...	minlūeñē.				
Prow ...	karū-he (*of a canoe*).						
Puff ...	... ...	... ...	nfâa (*blow*).				
Pull ...	duinde (*p- a paddle*). koang (*p- an our*).	duéd ...	tàak ...	... ...	gno-en (*in a canoe*).	arb-doé-ke-r e-kay.	
Pulse ...	... ...	... ...	hehæm; khiuk vha.				
Punch ...	... ...	... ...	... ...	... ...	... ...	(*O.H.B.*) dootka (*p- with fists*).	
Punish ...	... ...	... ...	hilēē.				
Pupil ...	... ...	... ...	khuan-kamūin.				
Pure ...	... ...	... ...	tschu.				
Pursue ...	... ...	... ...	hāhō.				
Put ...	... ...	... ...	hōta ...	... ...	... ...	thég-ge-ka (*p- down*).	
	... ...	... ...	té ...	... ...	... ...	(*O. H. B.*) itarec (*p- out a light*).	

Q.						
Quantity ...	... ...	... ...	karhé.			
Quarrel ...	... ...	... ...	... ...	... ...	... ...	arb-to' go kay.
Queenconque ...	tji-nal-rœ te kadu	wōk.				
Question ...	(*E.H.M.*) humma.					
Quick ..	loá ...	... ...	loto; lo-ēt ...	(*deRff.*) kajel ...	... ...	co'-roo (*be q-*).
Quiet ...	... ...	... ...	fo (*to quiet*) ...	... ...	... ...	arkundo'-do-kay (*quietly*). millo-kay(*beq-*).
Quill ...	anèt lébré; nai ka lang.					
R.						
Rabbit ...	... ...	... ...	kum't.			
Rage ...	... ...	... ...	khiank-fô-nâat.			
Rail ...	... ...	... ...	hēm, nlēn.			
Rain ...	amī ...	... ...	amé ...	(*deRff.*) kumra...	... ...	uméda.
	ami ti tong (*it rains*).	... ...	ju tong amé (*it rains*).	... ...	... ...	umé-la-par kay (*it rains*).
	mifaie (*a great rain*).	... ...	haming ...	... ...	... ...	jungda. (*O.H.B.*) yome.
Rainbow ...	kamindo kalœ.					
Rascal ...	... ...	... ...	hat-tulan-atse.			
Rasp ...	... ...	... ...	... ...	(*Gal.*) gunheel.		
Rat ...	(*Rosen*) komæt...	... ...	kum't.			
Rattan (189) ...	(189) nât.					
Raw (190) ...	(*E. H. M.*) hooyow	... ...	mahâa; uhehâa...	... ...	... ...	(190).
Ray ...	oshóa.					
Reach ...	... ...	... ...	theûn.			

The vowels are sounded as in German or Hindustani, *j* as *y* in 'yard;' *ei* and *ai* are sounded like 'eye;' *au* as in 'Auge' (German); *æ* as *ai* in 'fair;' *œ* as in 'Oel' (German); *ch* soft as *ch* in 'loch.'

188.—*E. H. Man.* '*Yahnai shehka; the natives do not recognize this word.*

189.—*Rosen.* '*Potáng;' E. H. Man, 'pantang.'*

190.—*Little Andaman, deRff., 'jiga.'*

English Words.	The Nancowry Dialect.	Great Nicobar.	Teressa by M. Plaisant.	Car Nicobar.	Inland race 'Shobængs.'	Andaman Words.	Remarks.
Read ...	anèt te lébré (*means also 'to write'*).	... ...	athuéta nèn pâhé hatulmi hathielké.	(*Gal.*) ahiet lebré	... ...	(*O.H.B.*) yapkă.	
Rear (191) ...	... ...	... ...	... ...	... ...	... ...	(191).	
Receive ...	... ...	... ...	hukét hukiét. khien.				
Reciproque ...	... ...	... ...	huleang.				
Red ...	âgh ...	... ...	sakiāh.				
Red-cloth ...	... ...	... ...	to ætva; sakalōt.				
Red-coral ...	(*A. C. M.*) iang mary.						
Reflect ...	... ...	... ...	admoot.				
Refuse ...	... ...	... ...	hatalāng; himegn.				
Regarding ...	... ...	... ...	pun; pu.				
Reject ...	... ...	... ...	kaveâgn; kavhe-hile.				
Reign ...	... ...	... ...	nhangatâat.				
Relative ...	... ...	... ...	akhui.				
Remain ...	katœv ...	... ...	... ...	... ...	... ...	(*O. H. B.*) bij-rēēka.	
Remove ...	... ...	... ...	lhotksi.				
Renumerate ...	hajuaha.						
Report ...	... ...	... ...	ghēn-kavipâhé.				
Reserve ...	... ...	... ...	honhâame.				
Resist ...	hat alâm; hatalang.						
Rest ...	... ...	... ...	hehang; hahiang nphé.	(*Gal.*) katu ...	... ...	(*O. H. B.*) a-ēr (*resting-place*).	
Retch ...	ho-ov (*vomit*) ...	... ...	... ...	... ...	o-œl (*vomit*).		
Retire ...	ferong.						
Return ...	sho-a-té-ré ...	... ...	sâth.				
Rib ...	tēn-jo-āk ...	... ...	heha ...	... ...	... ...	arparretarda.	
Rice (192) ...	(192) arōsh ...	... ...	aros ...	... ...	... ...	iat.	
Rich ...	(*Gal.*) baju-ta-khi-oaho. (*E. H. M.*) chum-woahon.	... ...	huheu.				

Right ...	... ...	... ...	loto hiâala. l'huhæhet.		
Ring ...	kalongtei (*finger ring*)	... ...	atlhāāt ...	(*Gal.*) kinloht, kinlong.	... ...	woolootartaékay (*ring a bell*).
Ripe ...	hemong ...	... ...	ivi himôn; himâan.		
	imong ...	... ...	ivi himâan.		
Rise ...	kaun-la-dé ... shoëka.	... ...	hahahmang ...	... ...	... ...	bo-e-kay.
River ...	(*Nov.*) hiajarak.				
Road (192A) ...	gadji (192A) ...	... ...	kai; kæi ... hûh'hægn'nkæt (*lose the road*).	... ...	... ...	thinga da. tangalēn. (*O.H.B.*) tinga.
Roast ...	harôk.					
Rock ...	... ...	... ...	patu-ta-karhû ...	... ...	... ...	talleda.
Roll ...	... ...	... ...	... ...	... ...	... ...	ogokay (*r- on the ground*).
Roof ...	aug gñee.					
Room ...	... ...	... ...	khiuk.			
Root ...	onjiha ...	... ...	heh't khiâ. hæh't khiâ.			
Rope ...	tanōka ...	... ...	kāmâpê-hehâahe pūrhon.	(*Gal.*) parhon ...	... ...	baith'moda. (*O.H.B.*) batma.
Rot ...	... ...	... ...	pahōhi (*to r.*) ... sakit-pahōhi (*rotten*).	... ...	... ...	(*O. H. B.*) mākā (*rotten*).
Rough ...	... ...	... ...	... ...	... ...	... ...	(*O.H.B.*) palair chainkdă (*it is rough*).
Round ...	kawæl-ing-a-dé	... ...	hat-râatk-nphé.			
Row ...	duinde (*paddle*) kannōt (*with an oar*).	... ...	... ...	... ...	... ...	etharparkay.
Rub off ...	... ...	... ...	... ...	... .	... ...	goo'-thookay.

The vowels are sounded as in German or Hindustani; *j* as *y* in 'yard;' *ei* and *ai* are sounded like 'eye;' *au* as in 'Auge (German); *æ* as *ai* in 'fair;' *œ* as in 'Oel' (German); *ch* soft as *ch* in 'loch.'

191.—*Little Andaman, deRff, 'minjoa' (go to the rear).*
192.—*Spanish 'arroz.'*

192A.—*F. E. T. 'Kai-ee.'*

English Words.	The Nancowry dialect.	Great Nicobar.	Teressa by M. Plaisant.	Car Nicobar.	Inland race 'Shobængs.'	Andaman Words.	Remarks.
Rudder ...	lāræla ...	... ...	... ...	... ...	... ...	(*O. H. B.*) argēēn.	
Run ...	tjeñg-ga ...	... ...	rhâgne ...	... ...	... ...	katsh-kay (*r- away.*)	
	di-eng-ga ...	... ...	rhigne ...	... ...	... ...	(*O. H. B.*) arwiteeka.	
Rust ...	het-a-i ...	... ...	... ...	... ...	... ...	kithékay.	
S.							
Sack ...	sajōw.						
Sacrifice ...	... ...	... ...	tahnihætsen.				
Sad ...	tjīt ...	... ...	... ...	... ...	... ...	boolupkay.	
Sail ...	hintæhe ...	... ...	ruhēn ...	... ...	... ...	otho joo mokay. ákangei (*go about in a canoe*).	
Salâm (193) ...	... ...	... ...	hahihalenma.				
Salt ...	shál. deâgh kammelæ. (*s- water*).						
Sand ...	piēt ...	... ...	... ...	... ...	... ...	tar'rada.	
Sardine (*or a little fish like it*).	tjafoin.						
Satisfied (194) ...	léat ...	... ...	... ...	... ...	... ...	(194) tickbootray.	
	pahaé ...	... ...	... ...	... ...	... ...	(*O. H. B.*) tirboot kâ. (*s—with eating*).	
Saw (*a s-*) ...	ganétal ...	... ...	pehang-khiâ.				

Say ...	oljole ...	... ...	hiheie, hehamang	... ...	... ...	mitji bada titankay (*what are you saying?*). (*O. H. B.*) mechebudda (*what are you saying?*).
Scale ...	... ...	... ...	hūk.			
Scent ...	hinshóv-é.					
Scissors ...	kanwāp.					
Scold ...	... ...	... ...	... ...	... ...	... ...	towoké. arbutju ullu ulizkay.
Scoop ...	to-i-deâgh.					
Scorpion ...	kolong-dea-napæ	ogñaula ...	... ...	... ...	... ...	thoóda.
Scraper (195) ...	(195) kanshei ...	... ...	akit (*to scr—*)			
Scratch ...	pishi	... ...	akit ...	... ...	... ...	(*O. H. B.*) raingutka.
Scream ...	... ...	... ...	tikâat kahehole. tikâat kahehâale.			
Screwpine (196) (*i. e., Pandanus*).	larôme (*the eatable*). (196) hikæ (*the wild one*).					
Sea (197) (198) ...	(197) kammelæ	... ...	nliôn ...	... ...	... ...	rath'-ar-da. joó-rar-da. (*O. B. B.*) polour chainkda (*the s- is rough*).

The vowels are sounded as in German or Hindustani; *j* as *y* in 'yard;' *ei* and *ai* are sounded like 'eye;' *au* as in 'Auge' (German); *æ* as *ai* in 'fair;' *œ* as in 'Oel' (German); *ch* soft as *ch* in 'loch.'

193.—*The common form of salutation in the East is 'salâm.'*
194.—*Little Andaman, deRff., 'mæmavel.'*
195.—*It is the thorny-leaf stem of a rattan, commonly used for domestic purposes. In places where they are not found (as for instance at Teressa,) these scrapers are imported at a high price.*
196.—*Rosen. 'Larôm.'*
197.—*Rosen. 'Goál-kamalæ.'*
198.—*Schowra, deRff., 'énléang.'*

English Words.	The Nancowry dialect.	Great Nicobar.	Teressa by M. Plaisant.	Car Nicobar.	Inland race 'Shobængs.'	Andaman Words.	Remarks.
Seahorse (*hippo-campus*).	mocongra.						
Search ...	... ...	... ...	haliet ...	... ...	... ...	(*O.H.B.*) atākă.	
Seat ...	... ...	... ...	... ...	... ...	... ...	(*O.H.B.*) dāmā (*the s—*)	
Seaweed ...	... ...	... ...	kamâpehehâahe.				
Secretly ...	... ...	... ...	huro-en hurohé.				
See ...	haróo ...	ho-a-ka ...	hahea.				
	hew ...	... ...	harea.				
Seed ...	op-æp.						
Seek ...	... ...	... ...	hukét hukiét.				
Seem ...	... ...	... ...	hoatse.				
Seldom ...	... ...	... ...	kăeæt.				
Self ...	... ...	... ...	tsie hæn.				
Sell (199) ...	(199) halau.						
Servant ...	... ...	... ...	khuan-kamūin.				
Set fire to ...	... ...	... ...	... ...	... ...	... ...	(*O.H.B.*) poo-cutkă.	
Seven	ishāt ... lué tafuél héang joang.	... ...	... ...	... ...	o-in.		
Seventeen	shaum ishāt. ishāt tafuél héang noang.						
Seventy	lué umdjomé ruktei. lué inein ruktei (*of nuts*). lué inein tanein tafuél.						
Several ...	... ...	... ...	hehor khui.				
Sew ...	itjé ...	... ...	... ...	... ...	... ...	jhart'-kay.	
Shade ...	... ...	... ...	rûhe (*shadow*)	... ...	... ...	(*O.H.B.*) jātkă. the'-arda.	
Shake ...	... ...	... ...	nghoik.				

Shark (200) ...	main.					
Sharpen ...	... ...	... ...	irat ...	... ...	... ...	orkojieth'kay.
Shave ...	kōha ...	... ...	katsi-khai ...	... ...	... ...	oth-jair-kay.
She ...	ánnæ ...	... ...	ané. nhæng, næn.			
Sheep ...	kaperæ.					
Sheet ...	lanōp ithéak (*bed sh—*)					
Shell (201) ...	(201) pugâ ; tim-bohé.	... ...	ehong ; enaii ...	... ...	... ...	(*O.H.B.*) odee.
	eleila(*king-conque*) shinalerœ(*rosebud*)	... ...	kalāā.			
Shellfish ...	aheôl ...	... ...	enrhui.			
Shin ...	hanang ...	... ...	hænañg.			
Shine ...	... ...	... ...	... ...	... ...	... ...	chor'-e-kay.
Ship	tjong ...	... ...	harâak kiong (*ship's cargo*).	... ...	he-at (*large sh—*)	
	tjong helein (*steamer*).					
	tjong hinkōk (*man of war*).	... ...	kiong ; tjiong. kiong invan (*man of war*).			
Shirt ...	kanhoin ; kanjūt.					
Shivering ...	... ...	... ...	khihahæt.			
Shoe ...	shapāta djanāpla.	... ...	renable.			
Shoot ...	haréle ...	... ...	fuhæn (*of a tree*)	(*Gal.*) harol ...	... ...	othpoo'-ge-en-kay.
			hahhewil ...	... ...	... ...	arb-pi'-de-kay.
			kana-khiâ (*of a tree*).	... ...	... ...	peit kay.
	... ...	... ...	... ...	... ...	... ...	(*O.H.B.*) paitka.
Shorten ...	... ...	... ...	peitæ-ivi.			
Short ...	me-æ-ho ...	... ...	mitæk.			
Shot (202) ...	(202) ahéol hindæl.					

The vowels are sounded as in German or Hindustani; *j* as *y* in 'yard;' *ei* and *ai* are sounded like 'eye;' *au* as in 'Auge' (German); *æ* as *ai* in 'fair;' *œ* as in 'Oel' (German); *ch* soft as *ch* in 'loch.'

199.—*Fontana.* '*Henvlej.*'

200.—*Rosen.* '*Ma-in.*'

201.—*Rosen.* '*Sin' algóeh.*' *Perhaps Mr. Rosen saw nothing but rose-buds.*

202.—*E. H. Man,* '*kutchung kutchung?*' *F. E. T.,* '*mong-haart.*'

English Words.	The Nancowry Dialect.	Great Nicobar.	Teressa by M. Plaisant.	Car Nicobar.	Inland race 'Shobængs.'	Andaman Words.	Remarks.
Shoulder (203) ...	ko-i-úngo. tjong-pak.						
Shoulder-blade ...	itjai.						
Show ...	(*E. H. M.*) hy-chung (*imperative*).	... ...	hahēha ...	... ...	... ...	tik-ba-de-kay.	
Shower ...	... ...	... ...	lampolci.				
Shrimp ...	shoang.						
Shut ...	ka-dop-ha-tá ...	... ...	âapn ; âaps. harhēha nlēn.				
Sick (204) ...	too ...	... ...	hahn'hâ (*sick fare*)	... ...	... ...	erbunggikay.	
	pomkeie ...	... ...	sakīt-pahōhi ...	... ...	... ...	(*O.H.B.*) ubā-trī (*s- ness*).	
Side ...	jafang ol hō-e (*this s—*) jafang ōl (*that s—*)						
Sigh ...	ejum ...	... ...	elum.				
Silence ...	... ...	... ...	... ...	... ...	... ...	mi-lan-ga-ké.	
Silver ...	... ...	... ...	para.				
Since ...	... ...	... ...	hæng.				
Sing ...	ikōshe ...	... ...	tikâat, tekâat ...	(*Gal.*) thckakh raave.	ejū ...	rar'-me-to-yo-kay. (*O.H.B.*) tooē-okă.	
Sister ...	tjau enkana (*elder s-*). tau enkana (*younger s-*).	... ...	... ...	... ...	... ...	adoati.	
Sit (205) (206) ...	pūjé (*s—down*)...	... ...	kiusset .. nkenēt.	... ...	gnide (*s—down*)	arkathoekay.	
Six ...	tafuel-6 ... lué tafuel (3 *pairs*).	... ...	... ...	... ...	lœv-ve.		
Sixteen ...	shaum tafuel. nfoan tafuel (8 *pairs*).						

Sixty ...	lué umdjomé. lué inein (*of nuts.*)					
Skin ...	ōka ...	... ...	hūk ... tafahole.	(*Gal.*) tahæ-æ ...	... ...	mo'-ro-da.
Sky ...	galahaie.					
Slander ...	(*E.H.M.*) kaiyon-nashee-paiyoo.	... ...	ghēn nel lopāh ka vipâhé.			
Slaughter ...	kalok.					
Sleep (207) ...	ithéak ...	komiñg ...	hitiak ; hitiak-té	(*Ham.*) loom-loom	gno-in ...	(207) marmekay.
Sleeve ...	koāla.		oplâap.			
Sling ...	... ...	... ...	hawnhōlĕt.			
Slipper ...	shapāta ...	... ...	renable.			
Small ...	tompænshé ...	... ...	... ...	... ...	... ...	kittimarda.
Smell (208) ...	(208) hæhæ ...	... ...	hah'k ...	... ...	... ...	noor'-oob-kay.
Smile ...	ité.					
Smith ...	dom ...	... ...	... ...	... ...	... ...	ar-ka-mo'-lar-da.
Smoke ...	adjīb (*the sm—*) top umhoin (*sm— of tobacco*).	... ...	ajùb ... aippe.	... ...	... ...	(*O.H.B.*) moula.
Snatch away ...	... ...	... ...	... ...	... ...	... ...	(*O.H.B.*) ekra.
Snake ...	peit (*poisonous sn—*) tulan (*Python Schneideri*). tjumléo (*sea-snake*).	... ...	pâit.			
Sneeze ...	e-a-e ...	... ...	héet ...	(*Gal.*) hiesse ...	... ...	orkonee'-lip-da.
Snore ...	he gno-ak.					
Soap ...	shavon.					
Softly ...	... ...	... ...	... ...	... ...	... ...	arkundo'-dokay.
Sole of foot ...	ol lá.					
Some ...	... ...	... ...	hatâap.			
Somebody ...	joang ...	... ...	ané pâhé. héang.			

The vowels are sounded as in German or Hindustani; *j* as *y* in 'yard;' *ei* and *ai* are sounded like 'eye;' *au* as in 'Auge' (German); *æ* as *ai* in 'fair;' *œ* as in 'Oel' (German); *ch* soft as *ch* in 'loch.'

203.—*Schowra, deRff., 'koipák.'*
204.—*Fontana, 'tohon;' E. H. Man, 'tchiak' (means 'pain').*
205.—*Schowra, deRff., 'po shé' ('sit down.')*
206.—*Little Nicobar, Galatea, 'kantai.'*
207.—*Little Andaman, deRff., 'mo-tæke.'*
208.—*E. H. Man. 'Eekait.'*

English Words.	The Nancowry dialect.	Great Nicobar.	Teressa by M. Plaisant.	Car Nicobar.	Inland race 'Shobængs.'	Andaman Words.	Remarks.
Some one ...	... ...	... ...	næt-hæt-umang.				
Some time ...	seju.						
Sometimes ...	(*E. H.* { kaiyai *M.*) { hanhang.	... ...	hiang hehe.				
Son ...	kōnje ...	... ...	khoin ...	... ...	kó-et.		
Son-in-law ...	(*Gal.*) konthje...	... ...	nkônhje khuan.				
Song ...	ikōshe ...	... ...	kintheu khiâ.				
Soon ...	mākā ...	... ...	mākā.				
Source ...	(*Hænsel.*) limpt.						
Sore ...	... ...	... ...	... ...	... ...	... ...	(*O.H.B.*) jāg.	
Sorrowful ...	... ...	... ...	kistot.				
Sorry ...	... ...	... ...	... ...	(*Gal.*) harihulong.			
Sort ...	... ...	... ...	mulōhe. tsie.				
Soul ...	... ...	... ...	mehaahet.				
Sound ...	... ...	... ...	hæng.				
Soup ...	kohelei; déagh-onang.						
Soup-ladle ...	hanæt-déagh. tajak tjoa.						
Sour ...	bagrein ...	... ...	hat tsiang (*not sweet*).	... ...	... ...	ar-rar-pij-da. ig-mor'-kar-da.	
South, (209) ...	(209) la-hgna.						
Sow ...	itjé ...	... ...	ikih loæt.				
Spade ...	... ...	... ...	... ...	... ...	... ...	(*O. H. B.*) ool.	
Speak ...	oljola ...	... ...	ghen.				
Spear, (*vide* Pig-spear).	*a—d* (*vide* Pig-spear). *e.* mia (*a little Neptune's-fork for fish*). *f.* hokpak (*a wooden many-pointed spear for little fish*)	*a. b. d.* (*vide* Pig-spear).	... ...	(*Gal.*) khova	*d.* (*vide* Pig-spear). *e.* kakang.		

Spew ...	ho-ow.					
Spider ...	kaleboie.					
Spine ...	henka.					
Spinster ...	holé-ang ...	... ...	... ...	(*deRff.* kekonje	... ...	arbjeddejog'-da.
Spirit ...	ivi *or* iwi ...	... ...	hivi. mehaahet.			
Spit ...	... ...	... ...	... ...	... ...	... ...	thoo'-bul-pe-kay.
Splendid ...	... ...	... ...	mâke.			
Split ...	(*F. E. T.*) oong tong.	... ...	mc-ik (*splendour*).			
Spoil ...	tajal.					
Spoon ...	shanćal (*big*) ... kanwi deâgh (*little.*)	... ...	sanam. sanam-nang (*ear-sp*—)			
Staircase ...	halak ...	... ...	tahia ...	(*Gal.*) tahiaal. (*Gal.*) tahja.		
Stammer ...	... ...	... ...	neole.			
Stand ...	(*Fontana*) achici-enga.	... ...	... ...	... ...	... ...	kar'-pekay.
Star (209 A) ...	shôkma ledja ...	... ...	... ...	... ...	... ...	chár-to-da.
Starry heaven ...	mifaie.					
Stay ...	katœv ...	... ...	... ...	... ...	... ...	par-le-kay. ker-wen-ni-do'-kay. (*O. H. B.*) brij-neekă.
Steamer ...	tjong helcín.					
Steal ...	(*F. E. T.*) koloch	... ...	... ...	... ...	... ...	(*O.H.B.*)tāpkă
Stepmother ...	... ...	... ...	nkînje ; pap.			
Stick ...	(*Gal.*) mhantje itjei (*ear-sticks*)	... ...	mhin.			
Stink ...	pa-œgñ.					

The vowels are sounded as in German or Hindustani; *j* as *y* in 'yard;' *ei* and *ai* are sounded like 'eye;' *au* as in 'Auge' (German); *æ* as *ai* in 'fair;' *œ* as in 'Oel' (German); *ch* soft as *ch* in 'loch."

209.—*Rosen.* '*Lang-sohông.*'

209*A.*—*Rosen.* '*Sjok-malîkja.*'

English Words.	The Nancowry Dialect.	Great Nicobar.	Teressa by M. Plaisant.	Car Nicobar.	Inland Race 'Shobængs.'	Andaman Words.	Remarks.
Stir ...	... ...	... ...	kutuhæ.				
Stockings ...	kanhole. djanapla.						
Stomach ...	wéang ...	... ...	viam ...	(*Gal.*) aithji ... karhû-viang (*thick-bellied*)	... ... /	(*O.H.B.*) jodo. (*O. H. B.*) tir-bootkă (*full st-*).	
Stomach-ache ...	*vide* Stomach *and* Ache.	... ...	khiak-viang.				
Stone ...	mañgæ ...	... ...	māngæ ...	... ...	... ...	tælida.	
Stool, 210 ...	... ...	... ...	... ...	... ...	... ...	210.	
Stoop ...	... ...	... ...	... ...	... ...	... ...	e-je-loth'-er-pe-kay.	
Stop ...	katœv ...	... ...	... ...	... ...	... ...	palikay. (*O. H. B.*) bij-reekă.	
Storm ...	... ...	... ...	sakalī ...	... ...	... ...	ainyarda.	
Stout ...	... ...	... ...	... ...	... ...	... ...	(*O.H.B.*) maj-ra (*not st-*).	
Straight ...	tæp-ha-dé ... tji um.	... ...	hoatse.				
Stranger ...	kalein. kaling.						
Stray ...	... ...	... ...	hûh'hæg'nkæt.				
Stream ...	... ...	... ...	... ...	... ...	... ...	ob'-da.	
Strew ...	... ...	... ...	heâgn ; hægn.				
Striped cloth ...	(*Font.*) camba-lamagn.						
String ...	fanũé.						
Stroke ...	... ...	... ...	nfhâ.				
Strong ...	koang ...	... ...	sakalu ; kalet ... haheng sakalu (*str—wind*). karhû-khugtot (*str- heart, i. e., love.*)	... ... /	... ... /	arb-go'-ra-da. arb-go'-ra-tho-gar-da (*very str-*)	

Stupid ...	(*E. H. M.*) had akai.						
Suffer ...	... ...	... ...	khiak.				
Sugar ...	sjunk ...	... ...	sukri.				
Sugarcane (211)...	(211) maœv ...	... ...	hāhaâ ...	... ...	... ...	ritaday (*new word*).	
Summer ...	hash fol (*north-east monsoon*).						
Sun (212) ...	(212) haĕng ...	... ...	híuk ...	... ...	... ...	bo'-do-da.	
Sunrise ...	al-hakī ...	... ...	aki akí ...	... ...	... ...	(*O.H.B.*) bodo. (*O.H.B.*) choe-kă.	
Supreme ...	... ...	... ...	... ...	... ...	... ...	thorma (*the Supreme Being*).	
Supposed ...	... ...	... ...	iana, ianet.				
Surely ...	... ...	... ...	rhâatk ; rhâalke.				
Surf ...	jōk.						
Surplus ...	... ...	... ...	tenam.				
Surprise ...	... ...	... ...	hukét ; hukiét.				
Surround ...	... ...	... ...	nlēn.				
Swallow (213) ...	(213) manlej-ñje (*a sw-*).	kinluch'si (*to sw-*)					
Swallows'nest ...	hikàe (*eatable*).						
Sweat ...	hō-āng.						
Sweep ...	efâ ...	... ...	fâ̂â ; fâ̂â-ifit ...	(*Gal.*) hetpati.			
Sweet ...	shéang ...	shetto ...	kuchiki ...	... ...	... ...	arnarda.	
	kobæng (*sw-potatoe*).	... ...	muite.				
	tjūng (*sweet water*).	... ...	tsiang.				
	taab deâgh (*sweet water*).	... ...	kuping-kalin (*sweet potatoes*). kamang-kalin (*sw-orange*).				

The vowels are sounded as in German or Hindustani ; *j* as *y* in 'yard ;' *ei* and *ai* are sounded like 'eye ;' *au* as in 'Auge' (German) ; *æ* as *ai* in 'fair ;' *œ* as in 'Oel' (German); *ch* soft as *ch* in 'loch.'

210.—*Little Andaman, deRff.*, '*minjoa.*'
211.—*Rosen.* '*Maágh.*'
112.—*Rosen.* '*Hæhn.*'
213.—*Rosen.* '*Enléhnja.*'

English Words.	The Nancowry Dialect.	Great Nicobar.	Teressa by M. Plaisant.	Car Nicobar.	Inland race 'Shobængs.'	Andaman Words.	Remarks.
Swim ...	ketjaldé ...	... ...	... ...	... ...	... ...	pitkay. potkay.	
Swine (214) ...	nōt ... shuruál (*wild sw-*).	... ...	... ...	(214) (*Ham.*) hown	... ...	rogo.	
Sword-blade ...	kidi ...	... ...	... ...	... ...	kakoat koi.		
T.							
Table (215) ...	(215) mæ-sje.						
Tail ...	dit ten ...	... ...	hehetsen.				
Take ...	okæ ... oræ.	... ...	hæle ...	... ...	... ...	ekay.	
Talk ...	oljōle ...	... ...	... ...	... ...	... ...	e-jan-kay. titānkay.	
Tall ...	(*E. H. M.*) tchong-koee. tching.	... ...	... ...	... ...	... ...	ob-lar-po-da.	
Tattie (*matted split bamboos*)	kandūla.						
Tattoo ...	... ...	... ...	... ...	... ...	... ...	kapi. aticka (*means also 'to write'*).	
Tea (216) ...	(216) tja ...	... ...	tschah.				
Teach ...	... ...	... ...	kistot. kom-ta-liap.				
Tear ...	... ...	... ...	tâakne (*t- asunder*)	... ...	... ...	par-rar-thar-kay.	
Tea-spoon ...	kanwi deâgh.						
Teaze ...	... ...	... ...	... ...	... ...	... ...	ig-noo'-loo-mud-kay.	
Teeth (217) ...	(217) kanap ...	... ...	... ...	... ...	... ...	e-thoog'-da mite-tog-day.	
Tell ...	oljōle ...	... ...	bihaie, hahamang	... ...	... ...	(*O. H. B.*) pur-chēkă.	
Temperance ...	... ...	... ...	hahn'hâ.				

Temples ...	hoáng.					
Ten (218) ...	shaum ... (218) shom ...	... ...	som ... son.	... ...	té.	
Tense ...	... ...	... ...	hé (*mark of the present tense*).			
Teressa ...	tatăt (*people of Schowra and Teressa*).					
Terror ...	pohoá.					
Testicula ...	mindja.					
That ...	anné ...	... ...	tēn; tīn.			
Theft ...	kalō ...	... ...	kalot.			
Thee ...	mæ ...	... ...	má; mén; meut. mæ; mæn; næg.			
Then ...	... ...	... ...	khă-it han.			
There (219) ...	(219) aná.	... ...	... ...	... ...	... ...	utshada.
They (220) ...	(220) anné ...	... ...	ané.			
Thick ...	di-joang.					
Thief ...	kalō ...	... ...	pâhé-ta-kalot ...	... ...	... ...	(*O.H.B.*) tāpkă.
Thigh ...	pulō ...	... ...	l'hæt pulô ... lækimâan.	... ...	... ...	(*O. H. B.*) pa-chudda.
Thin ...	... ...	... ...	... .	... ...	... ...	(*O.H.B.*) majră.
Thine ...	... ...	... ...	mēn.			
Think ...	... ...	... ...	admoot (*reflect*).			
Thirst ...	hæléang ...	... ...	hiliang ...	(*Gal.*) hilæang...	... ...	(*O.H.B.*) akair-kă. apanatjatkay.
Thirteen ...	shaum lué ... tafuél-tafuél héang noang.	... ...	sam-luæh.			
Thirty ...	héang umdjomeh ruktei.	... ...	tuktei hæng.			

The vowels are sounded as in German or Hindustani; *j* as *y* in 'yard;' *ei* and *ai* are sounded like 'eye;' *au* as in 'Auge' (German); *æ* as *ai* in 'fair;' *œ* as in 'Oel' (German); *ch* soft as *ch* in 'loch.'

214.—*Galathea, Car Nicobar, 'kahuhoke.'*
215.—*Malay; Fontana has 'cheráchà.*
216.—*Hindustani.*
217.—*Rosen. 'Kanâp.'*

218. *Revd. Barbe. 'Lam;' the natives must have been misunderstanding him.*
219.—*Novara. 'Matareo.' E. H. Man gives the same!*
220.—*E. H. Man. 'Oomtohm;' it means 'all'.*

English Words.	The Nancowry Dialect.	Great Nicobar.	Teressa by M. Plaisant.	Car Nicobar.	Inland race 'Shobængs.'	Andaman Words.	Remarks.
This ...	héang inein tanein tafuél (*of nuts*). ninné ... néó ...	... ...	ané; hiē; næn. nhæng; tsie næn (*as this*).				
Thorn ...	... ...	... ...	nōle.				
Thou ...	mæ-e ...	... ...	(*vide* Thee).				
Thousand ...	a umdjomé ruktei (*of nuts*). a inein tanein tafuél umdjomé.	... ...	samōng. s(*k*) aminâat (*thousand feet*).				
Thread ...	ehelō-e ... etjelō-e.	... ...	... ...	... ...	... ...	mor-ler-da.	
Three ...	lūé ...	... ...	loæh.				
Throat ...	kōl āle.						
Throw (221) ...	... ...	... ...	... ...	... ...	... ...	(221) (*O.H.B.*) dhāpeeka(*thr-away*).	
Thumb ...	mundúe ...	... ...	minrūa.				
Thunder ...	kom-doo-gña; (*F. E. T.*) lameean.						
Tide (221A) ...	tomda ... (*F. E. T.*) nāh (*low t-*). (*F. E. T.*) tomg-drah (*high t-*) (221A).	... ...	... ...	... ...	... ...	ella-airkay (*low t-*). ella-boo'kay (*high t-*). (*O.H.B.*) juru-chainkdā *high t-*). (*O.H.B.*) ulair-kā (*low t-*).	
Tie ...	(*F. E. T.*) al-tōäl	... ...	ilēnbe ... nlēn.	... ...	... ...	(*O.H.B.*) ronē-kă.	
Time ...	Iné shoa, (3 *times*)	... ...	a-khongat; khunh-je (2 *times*).	... ...	... ...	(*O.H.B.*)go-ē-lin (*the present t-*).	

Tin ...	perâta (*a-t-*).				
Tipsy ...	hujōé.				
Tired (222) ...	(*F. E. T.*) koh ...	... ...	... ...	... ...	(222.)
Tobacco (223) ...	umhóin pá (*China t-*).	... ...	fâ-kaiot; opt (l) âap.	... ...	henk tjerōin.
	umhóin komlām (*leaf-t*).	... ...	tahōng.		
Today ...	linhæng ...	... ...	næn hæng.		
Toddy ...	tó-ak ...	... ...	... ...	... ...	lahei.
Toe	kanélá. mundué (*big t—*) munshonka (*2nd t—*) munju-ung nie (*3rd t—*) tanue mendenje (*4th t—*) mendentjé (*5th t—*)				
Together ...	... ...	... ...	huleang.		
Tomorrow (224) ..	224 hakī ...	pentā ...	haghi; taki; ...	... ...	jabū ...	wine-ker-leck-da.
	seju lang (*the day after t—*)	... ...	takui shæh't (*the day after to-morrow*).	... ...	... ...	alaritkay. (*O. H. B.*) lit-teekă.
Ton ...	... ...	... ...	pipa.		
Tongue ...	galetâk ...	... ...	... ...	... ...	... ...	ar kar-eth-ilda. (*O. H. B.*) mo-tatoel.
Too ...	... ...	... ...	karhû-atse (*too much*).		
Tooth (*vide* Teeth).					
Toothpick ...	shôk kanap ...	... ...	sanam-kanâp.		
Top ...	... ...	... ...	khui. mang.		

The vowels are sounded as in German or Hindustani; *j* as *y* in 'yard;' *ei* and *ai* are sounded like 'eye;' *au* as in 'Auge' (German); *æ* as *ai* in 'fair;' *œ* as in 'Oel' (German); *ch* soft as *ch* in 'loch.'

221.—*Little Andaman, deRff.*, '*jalæ.*'
221*A*.—*Mr. Tuson's one word is evidently the same as mine.*
222.—*Little Andaman, deRff.*, '*benimange.*'
223.—*Schowra, deRff.*, '*pa.*'
224.—*Rosen.* '*Haghi.*'

English Words.	The Nancowry Dialect.	Great Nicobar.	Teressa by M. Plaisant.	Car Nicobar.	Inland Race 'Shobængs.'	Andaman Words.	Remarks.
Torch ...	pal.						
Tortoise ...	ok-tæ-e-ka ...	i-te-heng ...	... ...	... ...	athéak ...	(*O.H.B.*) taoo.	
Tortoise-shell (225) (226).	(225) ok kâp. op-kâp.	watow ...	... ...	... ...	mœ-auk ...	(226).	
Total ...	(*E. H. M.*) shin nama.						
Touch ...	... ...	... ...	hukét-hukiét.				
Towards ...	... ...	... ...	tēn ; tīn.				
Town ...	mattai ...	... ...	khiuk.				
Transgress ...	... ...	... ...	tan-hiâai.				
Travel ...	... ...	... ...	... ...	... ...	... ...	(*O.H.B.*) naukă.	
Tree (227) ...	(227) o-gni'-ha ...	... ...	fhuhæn (*shoot of tree*).	... ...	... ...	arrineda.	
	kametjol (*a tr- with white leaves*).	... ...	khiâ ...	... ...	... ...	tāng.	
	jong-o-jav (*cocoa-nut tr-*).					darrine leek-now-lar'-kay *go up a tr-*).	
	komtjing (*ebony*).						
Trepang (*Holothuria*).	(Rosen) toit.						
Triangle ...	... ...	... ...	luæhman.				
Trigger ...	panōt hindæl.						
Trowsers (228) ...	kanha.						
Trough ...	holshôal.						
Truly ...	... ...	... ...	rhâatk, rhâalke.				
Truth ...	... ...	... ...	... ...	... ...	... ...	ar-thad'-e-kay.	
Tumbler ...	la hetwâ wæteræ. ...	... ...	nphâ-kinmæle.				
Turban ...	leinshi ...	... ...	kerebusse. tanâan khuī.				
Tureen ...	petiñg.						
Turn ...	... ...	... ...	... ...	... ...	... ...	i-ji-gair-bul-kay.	

Turpentine (229)	(229) tæl.					
Turtle ...	kâp (*sea t—*) ... oktæeka (*land t—*)	... ...	kâp ...	... ...	... ...	jædi. yar-the-da. (*O.H.B.*) ya-dee. towda (*small*). garida.
Turtle-dove ...	tjumōa ...	... ...	kahàak.			
Twelve ...	shaum-ā ... tafuél-tafuél.	... ...	sam-ôh.			
Twenty ...	héang inein (*of nuts*) héang umdjomé.	... ...	hâtianan-tœn.			
Twist ...	lei-gna.					
Two ...	ā ... héang tafuél.	... ...	oh, æh ...	... ...	ā.	
U.						
Ugly (230) ...	(230) (*Nov.*) jooh	... ...	paat.			
Umbrella ...	hando-goi ...	... ...	nrōng-khūi.			
Umpire ...	... ...	... ...	pâhé-ta-ghēn.			
Uncertain ...	... ...	... ...	sak'n.			
Uncle (231) ...	hotjié ...	... ...	pap.			
Under ...	... ...	... ...	kata.			
Underarm ...	tji koál.					
Understand ...	léap ...	... ...	akah-eang (*eng ; iang*).			
Undermost ...	... ...	... ...	hakté.			
Uneven ...	tjong det.					
Unhappy ...	(*E.H.M.*) kit-ya-natau.					
Unite ...	... ...	... ...	hâahé.			

The vowels are sounded as in German or Hindustani: *j* as *y* in 'yard;' *ei* and *ai* sounded like 'eye;' *au* as in 'Auge' (German); *æ* as *ai* in 'fair;' *œ* as in 'Oel' (German); *ch* soft as *ch* in 'loch.'

225.—*Note the different pronunciation from 'bite,' where the last syllable is short.*

226.—*Little Andaman, deRff., 'nadélange.'*

227.—*Hænsel. 'Uniga.'*

228.—*Schowra, deRff., 'henjōt.'*

229.—*From the Hindustani.*

230.—*E. H. Man. 'Oomeh had shekka.*

231.—*Schowra, deRff., 'jōol-noāng.'*

English Words.	The Nancowry dialect.	Great Nicobar.	Theressa by M. Plaisant.	Car Nicobar.	Inland race 'Shobængs.'	Andaman Words.	Remarks.
Unjust ...	... ...	... ...	hat-tulan-atse. hat-tulan-ten-pâhé.				
Unkind ...	... ...	... ...	... ...	... ...	... ...	orkothicjarbug-da.	
Unmarried ...	... ...	... ...	... ...	... ...	... ...	(*O.H.B.*) abara.	
Unripe ...	gñæ-e ...	... ...	... ...	... ...	... ...	poo-thoong-ar-da.	
Untie ...	ejá.						
Untruthful ...	... ...	... ...	hat-tulan-atse.				
Up ...	... ...	... ...	... ...	... ...	... ...	kalageada. dar'-rine-leek-now-larkay (*go up a tree*). o'choo-thoon (*move up*).	
Up ...	... ...	... ...	metam.				
Utensil ...	... ...	... ...	... ...	... ...	... ...	(*O.H.B.*) booj (*cooking ut-*).	
V.							
Valley ...	alhōda.						
Value ...	... ...	... ...	vathâat.				
Vapour ...	... ...	... ...	fââklet.				
Vary ...	... ...	... ...	hahehôk.				
Vein ...	ehæ ...	... ...	hæhe ; tahæ.				
Very ...	... ...	... ...	... ...	... ...	... ...	arb-go'-ratho'-garda (*v-strong*).	
Vessel ...	tjong (*vide* Ship)	... ...	tjong ...	(*Gal.*) djugar (*drinking vessel of bamboo*).			
Victuals ...	auk nôk ...	... ...	hātnâak. kaiñt.				
View ...	... ...	... ...	haheam.				
Village (232) ...	(232) mattai ...	... ...	khiuk-njēē. matahæt.				

Virtue ...	... ...	... ...	hoatse.			
Vomit ...	ho-ov ...	... ...	sahuat.			
Voyage (233) ...	(233) (*Nov.*) yoha-tayha.					
W.						
Wages ...	hajúaha.					
Waistcoat ...	kanjut-tit-koála	... ...	kapap.			
Wait ...	pænteréjen ... katœv.	... ...	... ...	... ...	... ...	tantok milla-kay.
Wake ...	... ...	... ...	... ...	... ...	... ...	ai'-bul-kay. le'-ar-kay.
Walk (233A) ...	Font. hanscioun-ga (233A.)	... ...	kusang'n.			
	(*F.E.T.*) on-shon-gha.	... ...	mifā-æ.			
Want ...	jo; jetôt ... jetôt.	... ...	... ...	... ...	o-a-o ...	tar-tup-pu-ké.
War ...	pomôn ...	... ...	pamoiñ.			
War-hat ...	kam-mi-lī ...	... ...	(*kerebusse-teñ pamoiñ.*)			
Warm ...	kéojen; teien ...	... ...	hēn; tanhje.			
	okpâkteâk; tan-jaha.	... ...	hukhâahe.			
Warmth ...	... ...	... ...	amho-in.			
Warrior ...	(*E. H. M.*) hoo-ekka.					
Wash	jokoleit (*wash the body*).	... ...	akhik (*w—linen*)	(*Gal.*) tsiekite-sethj.	... ...	(*O.H.B.*) chat-ka (*bathe*).
	etjit (*w—cloth*).	... ...	tohiæn-atê {(*wash*,			
	tjaneit dāi (*w—hands*).	... ...	tohiæki-te {*bathe*)			

The vowels are sounded as in German or Hindustani; *j* as *y* in 'yard;' *ei* and *ai* are sounded like 'eye;' *au* as in 'Auge' (German); *æ* as *ai* in 'fair' *œ* as in 'Oel' (German); *ch* soft as *ch* in 'loch.'

232.—*Rosen.* '*Matta-i.*'
233.—*E. H. Man has the same with transposition, viz*; '*yotahayha.*'

233*A.*—*Both are evidently the same word* (1778 *and* 1874).

English Words.	The Nancowry Dialect.	Great Nicobar.	Teressa by M. Plaisant.	Car Nicobar.	Inland Race 'Shobængs.'	Andaman Words.	Remarks.
Wasp ...	kaléhaue.						
Watch ...	heang jang nang ...	... ...	nehang-nang ...	(*Gal.*)enhangnang.			
Water (234)	deâgh ...	... ...	dheâkh ...	māk ...	dūi (*fresh w-*)	(234) inarda.	
	fau dâgh (*sweet w-*)	... ...	... ...	... ...	le-it (*salt w-*)	inada.	
	deâgh kammelæ (*salt w-*)	... ...	... ...	... ...	... ...	(*O. H. B.*) ena.	
Water-bottle ...	jangmat.						
Waterholdy ...	... ...	... ...	reaksnān.				
Water-jug ...	tajak.						
Water-shells (*polished cocoa-nutshells.*)	hisbóje.						
Water-sticks (*to carry the water shells.*)	ido deâgh ...	... ...	... ...	(*Gal.*) shankal.			
Wave ...	jòk ...	... ...	hahek ...	... ...	... ...	par'-thar-rar-da.	
Wax ...	manjāk ...	... ...	maniak ...	... ...	... ...	ar'-ja-peej'-da.	
Way ...	gadji.						
We ...	tjūā ...	... ...	hââi ; hufæt. khiuh't.				
Weak ...	(*E. H. M.*) had-koang	... ...	... ...	... ...	... ...	arb-mar'-li-da.	
Weapon ...	(*vide* Gun, Bow, Spear).	... ...	kirhi. nehaurle.				
Weed ...	... ...	... ...	kamâpe-hehâahe (*sea w-*)				
Weep ...	tjim ...	... ...	bahuæie ...	(*Ham.*) poing.			
Weigh ...	(*E. H. M.*) kunlah.						
Well ...	katjoat (*a w-*)	... ...	lopah (*good*).				
West (235) ...	(235) shohōng	... ...	lakapah. kapah.				
Wetnurse ...	... ...	... ...	nkênhje-manam.				
Whale ...	... ...	... ...	karah.				

What (235A)	... ...	... ...	kun, ki, kô (*Acc.* kun, ka	... ...	... ...	mieh-e-bar-da (*wh- is it*).
	(*F. E. T.*) kin-kee-en ?	... ...	... ...	... ...	... ...	mitji-bada titankay (*wh—are you saying*).
	... ...	... ...	... ...	... ...	... ...	(*O.H.B.*) meche buddă (*wh—are you saying*).
When ...	kabæ ...	... ...	i a n a ; i a n e t ; khāæt.	... ...	... ...	wain-ga-li.
Where ...	joa ...	... ...	khuæt ; kuæt. khiuk ...	... ...	... ...	tanchor'-da. (*O. H. B.*) tin-rinee (*wh- do you live*).
Which ...	... ...	... ...	(*vide* What.)			
Whisker ...	anhoin.					
Whistle ...	tjanéong; hinfæp.					
White	téjen ...	... ...	longhaât (*wh-cloth*).	Gal. disso ...	... ...	tala-og-da.
	mō-ho-já (*wh—of an egg.*)	... ...	... ...	... ...	... ...	(*O. H. B.*) too-lea (*wh- hair*).
Whither ...	... ...	... ...	... ...	... ...	... ...	tintja.
Who ...	... ...	... ...	(*vide* What).			
Whole ...	omtohm.					
Whore ...	henj-enkana.					
Why (235A) ...	(*F. E. T.*) kyou-ja ? (235A).	... ...	kūn-hiâ ; kūn tsie.	... ...	... ...	mieh'-e-barda.
Wick ...	... ...	... ...	kanâme.			

The vowels are sounded as in German or Hindustani; *j* as *y* in 'yard;' *ei* and *ai* are sounded like 'eye;' *au* as in 'Auge' (German); *æ* as *ai* in 'fair;' *œ* as in Oel' (German); *ch* soft as *ch* in 'loch.'

234.—*Little Andaman, deRff., 'in-ô-ja.' The few words I have got of this language I learnt from a boy who was some months ago made a prisoner. He was put in my charge, but while he was with me he pined away. He was always sitting in the verandah looking down from 'Mount Harriett', which overlooks several islands. He fixed on some low islands on the West coast as his country and wanted always to go there. I never understood the passage (Judges vii. 5) 'Every one that lappeth of the water with his tongue, as a dog lappeth', till I saw him drink. He did that. He died after a short stay at Port Blair.*

235.—*Rosen. 'Suhôn.'*

235A.—*The mark of interrogation is Mr. Tuson's own.*

English Words.	The Nancowry dialect.	Great Nicobar.	Teressa by M. Plaisant.	Car Nicobar.	Inland race 'Shobængs.'	Andaman Words.	Remarks.
Wicked ...	... ...	... ...	hat-tsiaug.				
Wife ...	ñkañ	... ...	nkênhje; nkanhje.				
Wind	hāé ...	... ...	haheng. vi-khiuk-haheng (*to air*). haheng sakalu (*strong w-*).				
Wine ...	wiinje ...	... ...	taram.				
Wine-glass ...	wétéró.						
Wing ...	danoajo ...	... ...	nfaré ...	... ...	... ...	e'-gar-char-tar-da.	
Winter ...	shohong (*south-west monsoon*).						
Wipe ...	... ...	... ...	fââ, fââ-ifit.				
Wish ...	tōt ...	... ...	hehomang. hehōt.				
Woman (236 A) (236 B).	engkána ...	... ...	angana ...	(236 A) (*Ham.*) kecanna.	(236B) oju tjé-ang (*girl*).	appaila. (*O. H. B.*) abara (*unmarried*). (*O. H. B.*) abchabil (*married.*)	
	angkána ...	... ...	nkênhje.				
Wonder ...	... ...	... ...	lhâak.				
Wood ...	ogniha.						
Word ...	... ...	... ...	iang-ta-ghēn.				
Work (237) ...	(237) wæ ...	... ...	huhé; huhomi ... kuuvi kunhuhomi.	(*Gal.*) hatæiæh.			
World ...	... ...	... ...	matahæt ...	... ...	... ...	ar'rəmalathoó-rooda.	
Worm ...	... ...	... ...	karan. maleng.				
Worship ...	... ...	... ...	athiēlke; hatiēl-me. hisōsi athiēlke.				

Wound ...	wā-an ; wah ...	... ...	... ...	... ...	... ...	(*O. H. B.*) jāg.
Wrath ...	... ...	... ...	menam.			
Wreath (*of bast*) .	... ...	... ...	datjāājelāh.			
Wretched ...	... ...	... ...	fhôt.			
Wrestle ...	... ...	... ...	... ...	... ...	... .	arth-lai'-kay.
Wrist ...	lagá koál.					
Write (238) ...	(238) anèt te lebré	... ...	hatel ...	... ...	... ...	(*O. H. B.*) aticka (*means originally 'to tattoo'*).
Y.						
Yams (239) (240)	(239) kobeng ...	... ...	kuping ... tahula.	(*Gal.*) t'owla ...	... ...	(240.)
Yawn ...	tig-nāp ... hināp.	... ...	fââb.			
Year (241) ...	(241) som-en-jū ...	... ...	sâht. saminiūs, sāht.			
Yellow (242) ...	(242) gño ; gñœ.					
Yes ...	shía ; jo ...	... ...	hàh ; hâaht ...	... ...	... ...	orno ?
Yesterday ...	manjūé.					
Yet ...	... ...	... ...	abhi.			
Yolk ...	laharòme. laharòman.					
You ...	mæ-é ...	... ...	má, mēn ; meut...	... ...	... ...	ungola.
			mæ ; mæn ; næg .	... ...	... ...	angola.
Young ...	towæledo ... ilu (*unmarried*).	... ...	... ...	gni-e.		
Your (243) ...	(243) te-mæh ...	... ...	mēn. tsang-mæ.			

The vowels are sounded as in German or Hindustani ; *j* as *y* in 'yard ;' *ei* and *ai* are sounded like 'eye' ; *au* as in 'Auge' (German) ; *æ* as *ai* in 'fair' ; *œ* as in 'Oel' (German) ; *ch* soft as *ch* in 'loch.'

236 *A.—Galathea. 'Hikanna.'*
236 *B.—Shobæng, de Rff. 'Ojú bashói,' (boy) was omitted under Boy.*
237.—*E. H. Man, 'winnair shisleh;' doubtful.*
238.—*Fontana. 'Athebet;' E. H. Man, has only the two first syllables, viz., 'at ait.'*
239.—*Rosen. 'Kuping.'*

240.—*Little Andaman, de Rff. 'melotani.' I showed the Little Andaman prisoner some sweet potatoes and he at once and distinctly called it 'Nacobar tamati.' I expect they have visited Car Nicobar from Little Andaman.*
241.—*Their year is a monsoon and they have two to our year.*
242.—*Novara. 'Laaom,' so also E. H. Man.*
243.—*E. H. Man. 'Tchiangchier.'*

NUMERALS.

The Nicobarese have a system of counting different from ours. They count by twenties and four hundreds. Up to twenty they count by pairs, *e. g.*, 4 pairs *plus* 1=9; but also as we do up to ten, and then ten one, ten two and so on up to twenty. In counting by pairs they add a word at the uneven numbers between the word 'héang' (*i. e.* 'one') and the word that gives the thing they are talking of. Below I have given some instances, and the word in Italics is the word I am talking of, and which is different for different things.

Héang tafuel héang *ha* gni (one pair one *piece* house=3 houses).
A tafuel héang *noang* gnoat (5 cocoanuts).
Lué tafuel héang *joang* paju (7 men).
Fuan tafuel héang *tak* para (9 Spanish dollars).
Tanein tafuel héang *danōé* dué (11 canoes).

Of nuts they use the word 'inein' for 'twenty,' 'umdjomé' 'for four hundred.' Of other things they use 'umdjomé' for 'twenty' and put 'héang inein umdjomé' to mean 'four hundred' (1 by 20 by 20). 'Tafuel' means one pair but also six. The numerals are as below :—

English Numerals.	Nancowry dialect.	Teressa by M. Plaisant.	Car Nicobar.	Inland race 'Shobængs.'	Remarks.
One	héang	½=la imiang (*First*) 1=iang.	... ...	hing.	
Two	a ... ... héang tafuel.	oh, æh	... ...	a.	
Three	lué ... ... héang tafuel héang.	loæh	... ...	luge.	
Four	fuan ... ... a-tafuel.	foue, fen ...	... ...	fu et.	
Five	tanein ... ... a tafuel héang	tani	(*Gal.*) ta-nein ...	tein.	

Six	tafuel lué tafuel.	...	...	lœv-ve.
Seven	ishat lué tafuel héang.	...	...	oin.
Eight	nfuan fuan tafuel.	nfoon	(*Gal.*) hævret	taw-we.
Nine	héang hata fuan tafuel héang.	...	(*Gal.*)-kinteræ	nog-in.
Ten	shaum; shom tanein tafuel.	som, son	...	te.
Eleven	shaum héang tanein tafuel héang.	iang-tôn iaeang.		
Twelve	shaum a tafuel tafuel.	iang-tôn-haha.		
Thirteen	shaum lué tafuel tafuel héang.	iang-tôn-luæ.		
Fourteen	shaum fuan ishat tafuel.	iang-tôn-foue.		
Fifteen	shaum tanein ishat tafuel héang.	iang-tôn-tani.		
Twenty	heang inein (*of huts*) heang umdjomé.	hitianan-tön.		
Thirty	heang inein tanein tafuel (*of nuts*) heang umdjomé ruktei.	tuktei-hæng.		
Fourty	a inein (*of nuts*) a umdjomé.	fue-tôn.		
Fifty	a inein tanein tafuel (*of nuts*) a umdjomé ruktei.	tani-tôn.		
Eighty	fuan inein (*of nuts*) fuan umdjomé.			
Ninety	fuan inein tanein tafuel (*of nuts*) fuan umdjomé ruktei.			
One Hundred	tanein inein (*of nuts*) tanein umdjomé.	iang nang.		
Two Hundred	shaum inein (*of nuts*). shaum umdjomé.			
One Thousand	a umdjomé ruktei (*of nuts*) a inein ruktei umdjomé.	samōng.		

TIME.

The Nancowry people reckon by years (*som-en-jū*), each year consisting of one monsoon, so that two of their years make one of ours. The year is divided into moons (*kahæ*) subdivided by quarters of the moon. They very carefully follow the changes of the moon, mainly because they are great fishermen and are often out the greater part of the night fishing by torchlight, taking advantage of the low tides. They also watch the monsoons very keenly, as during the long rainy-season (*sho-hong*) all business stops. In the dry-season the trading vessels arrive, and at this time of the year the Nicobarese cross in their light canoes from one island to another. Beyond the present and nearest future time they take no heed. They do not know their age and can only refer to some event, such as 'Dr. Rosen's time,' to indicate any period of years ago. With regard to the divisions of the day they are very exact, but these divisions vary slightly, nevertheless, as they have neither clock nor sundial. I have not fixed the corresponding time after European reckoning, because I am not quite certain on the point, as the only clock which was in the Settlement is here no longer.

DAY (HENG OR HÆNG.)	NIGHT (HATAM.)
al hakī (*sunrise*).	shup heng (*sunset*).
kohin doáha (*forenoon*).	ladíejé (*dusk*).
kohin doáha (*later*).	pujue (*7 p. m.* ?)
ehala kam (*later*).	engshe heam auk nôk (*8 p. m.* ?)
kāmheng (*noon*).	heam auk nôk kā (*9 p. m.* ?)
shadie hehéng (*afternoon*).	heam auk nôk kéjau (*10 p. m.* ?)
tjin foatje tjong (*later*).	engshe joáng hatam (*11 p. m.* ?)
tjin foatje kā (*later*).	joáng hatam (*midnight*).
heng imat mito-e (*later*).	hahohaka kájau ka (*3 a. m.* ?)
heng imat kā (*later*).	puju (*5 a. m.* ?)
engshe shup heng (*just before sunset*).	tjangiol (*before sun appears*).

'Yesterday' is *manjúe*, 'today' *linheng*, 'tomorrow' *haki*, 'the day after tomorrow' *sejúlang*, while *seju* means 'later,' 'afterwards.' *Heng* means 'sun' and 'day;' they count by suns, hence the expression. The great divisions of human life are *kanjom*, 'child;' *ilú*, 'bachelor' (*i. e.*, marriageable); *paju*, 'the man who has a son;' *pomoeschæ*, 'old man;' *omiáh*, 'chief,' is also used of old men to designate them as such; '*bagro koi*,' with a little raillery in it, points to the grey hair of the old man.

A full-grown Nancowry man stands between 5 feet 6 inches to 5 feet 9 inches, the Andamanese between 4 feet 9 inches and 5 feet 1 inch.

N. B.—Any corrections, additions or notes that bear on the islands or their population will be thankfully received and will in any future edition be duly acknowledged.

O. S. G. P.—No. 68 H. D.—30-1-75.—300.